EVERY-DAY-OF-THE-SCHOOL-YEAR
MATH PROBLEMS

More Than 300 Quick, Incredibly Fun Activities
Linked to Each School Day

by Marcia Miller and Martin Lee

S C H O L A S T I C
PROFESSIONAL BOOKS

NEW YORK • TORONTO • LONDON • AUCKLAND • SYDNEY
MEXICO CITY • NEW DELHI • HONG KONG

To Matthew, a July birthday boy,
and his big sister Rachel,
who was born on a blue moon in May

Cover design by Jaime Lucero
Cover illustration by Jo Ann Adinolfi
Interior design by Solutions by Design, Inc.
Interior illustration by Izu Watanabe

ISBN 0-590-64407-6

CONTENTS

INTRODUCTION

THE ACTIVITIES

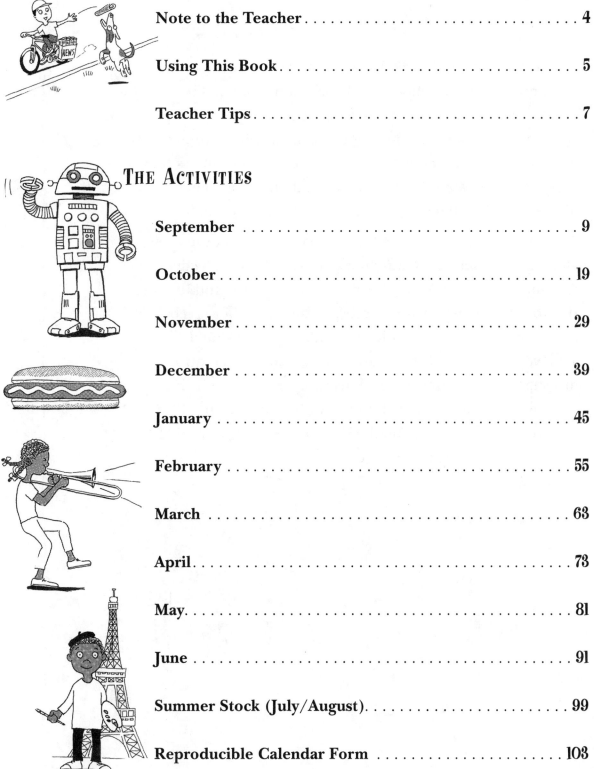

Dear Teacher,

Mathematics isn't something that happens in isolation for 45 minutes a day in school. Math—authentic math—is everywhere! It's woven into our language, into our conceptual thinking, into our daily routines, even into our entertainment. But children may not believe this unless they experience the abundance of math in their world. That's where *Every-Day-of-the-School-Year Math Problems* can help.

Every-Day-of-the-School-Year Math Problems is a light hearted almanac of quick ideas, nifty puzzlers, and exciting activities for almost every day of the year. It's fun, it's easy, and it's *real*. It's not as comprehensive as a formal almanac, but it *is* based on real events, actual people, and milestones of human achievement. Use this book as a springboard for creative investigations and open-ended discussions that can bring some whimsy into your curriculum while challenging children to rely on their math skills to predict, build, connect, invent, hypothesize, conclude, and summarize.

Here's to a great year!

Marcia Miller & Marty Lee

USING this BOOK

I n its *Curriculum and Evaluation Standards for School Mathematics,* the National Council of Teachers of Mathematics (NCTM) encourages a move toward building mathematical literacy in today's fast-changing world of information. The NCTM takes the ideal stance that students should learn to value mathematics, become confident in their ability to do mathematics, become mathematical problem solvers, learn to communicate mathematically, and learn to reason mathematically.

Of course, there is no one simple way to achieve such lofty goals. But one approach that seems to work is to present authentic questions that have some relevance to children's lives. So why not make daily life itself the subject of such challenges?

Nearly every classroom in the country has a calendar posted in it—teacher-made or commercial. Many school days begin with an acknowledgment of significant events of that day, such as birthdays, holidays, seasonal events, or historical milestones. These connections can bring a class together as a group and may direct the course of research or a unit of study. That's where *Every-Day-of-the-School-Year Math Problems* comes in.

For each month, each week of the month, and many individual days of the month, we've identified a fact, a birthday, an anniversary, a festival, or a celebration that can spark student interest. We have posed a mathematical query or challenge that students can answer based on that information. All questions have answers, even the more open-ended ones; but we don't always provide them. That's because the investigations will vary with the age of your students, the year you use the book, the location of your school or community, the sophistication of your class, and the depth to which you choose to plumb the subject. It's up to you to help students recognize the math embedded in every question and to apply a suitable technique, skill, or solution method that will yield a reasonable answer.

Most important, questions should pique students' curiosity and tantalize them to ask more questions. We hope they will wrestle with how to get their minds around a problem, how to break it into manageable parts, how to work through it, how to explain their plan of action and solution, and how to justify that it all makes sense.

In so doing, children will behave like *real* mathematicians.

Every-Day-of-the-School-Year Math Problems follows a regular monthly pattern starting with September, the month that most schools begin instruction. Within each of the ten full months (September through June), you'll find these features:

By the MONTH: Each month opens with a page of broad activities you can do anytime that month to echo a particular event, such as International Calendar Awareness Month or National Chicken Month. Sample activities include compiling a cookbook for a featured food, gathering and displaying data related to the theme, or taking measurements over time. Each month page ends with a list of other monthly events to incite your curiosity, but no specific ideas are suggested.

By the WEEK: Next, there are two pages of weeklong events, such as Home for Birds Week or Golden Rule Week. Some of these events are featured with several ways to explore them, others are simply listed for your information.

By the DAY: Then come the daily events, such as Sandwich Day, the birthday of a notable person, or an anniversary in history. You'll find a question, inquiry, project, or activity for every day of the school year.

SUMMER STOCK: Although most schools aren't in session during July and August, many teachers and families are interested in summertime learning. You may be in the habit of sending home a packet of recommendations families can explore together over the long break. "Summer Stock" is the feature in this book that addresses this need. It offers a handful of summer ideas you may suggest.

Finally, there is a reproducible blank calendar form you can use however you see fit. (Page 103)

Note: Many events fall on the same date every year. Others move, falling on, say, the third Tuesday of April or the first Monday in March. Still others are based on lunar calendars or other annual cycles that vary. We have tried to be as accurate as possible with our dates.

Resources: Some standard reference materials provide directories of annual events. One excellent source is *Chase's Calendar of Events,* which comes out each year. *The Guinness Book of Records,* another annual publication, is also useful. You can also access searchable databases on the Internet. Two valuable sites are http://www.historychannel.com/today and http://www.scopesys.com/anyday.

TEACHER TIPS

⊚ Not every question is appropriate for every class. Pick and choose as you see fit, and adapt questions as needed. For instance, if a question involves a local zoo and there are none in your vicinity, work with data from famous zoos, such as the San Diego Zoo or the Bronx Zoo, which have public relations departments that can provide the information you need.

⊚ You may discover an activity that meshes perfectly with your lesson plans, but not on its official day. No problem! Just use it whenever it works best.

⊚ Most questions lend themselves to collaboration and cooperative learning. Feel free to determine the best grouping to suit your teaching style, the learning styles of your students, and their levels of independence. You can examine most questions as a whole class or in groups, or assign them to individuals or pairs.

⊚ Encourage children to record their calculations, sketches, and solution plans in their math logs. Some activities might be appropriate for inclusion in students' math portfolios.

⊚ Use questions as class work, homework, or project work. You might open a math class with a question as a warm-up activity, or "Problem of the Day," or give a question as a homework assignment.

⊚ For questions with multiple answers, allow time for students to share their findings and solution methods with the class or in groups. As students share their findings, encourage them to acknowledge and respect the variety of methods and presentations that emerge. Because strategies can be so diverse, the quality of outcomes may vary. Enhance critical thinking by modeling how to question incomplete solutions or conclusions that don't seem to fit the facts.

⊚ Take time to join an investigation yourself. Students will benefit from seeing you in the role of investigator. They'll realize that there are things you don't know but can figure out by planning and following a sensible course of action. Ask questions and give hints. Aim students in the right direction.

⊚ Involve parents! Present calendar questions at parent meetings to demonstrate one more approach within your math program. Some questions may be ideal for workshops to help parents grasp the value of this kind of problem-solving.

⊚ Duplicate the Summer Stock pages and hand them out to students as the school year ends. Parents may appreciate having some concrete math activities their kids can work on over the summer.

SEPTEMBER by the MONTH

Many people see September as a month of beginnings: the start of a new school year, the advent of the Jewish New Year, the opening of new cultural seasons in theatre and the arts. But that's not all. September is—

⊚ **National Chicken Month**
Work with students to select, prepare, and eat easy dishes using chicken. Examples might include chicken tacos, chicken soup, or chicken salad. Plan a lunch of chicken soup with rice and mushrooms to honor three of September's monthlong food celebrations. Or create a class cookbook of chicken recipes. Focus on measuring ingredients, calculating numbers of servings, determining preparation and cooking times, total or cost per serving, and so on.

⊚ **National Piano Month**
This event honors the piano—America's most popular instrument. Over 20 million of us tickle the ivories. Take a survey to see how many students in your class play the piano or other instruments. Present findings in the form of a graph or chart. Or examine mathematical relationships among note values. Children who read music can draw whole notes, half notes, quarter notes, and eighth notes, and explain how they work together to form musical patterns. Pianists can demonstrate on a school piano or electronic keyboard.

⊚ **American Heritage Month**
Did you know that "United States" became our official name on September 9, 1776? September was also the month of other significant milestones in our nation's history. The formal end to the Revolutionary War came when the British and Americans signed a peace treaty in Paris on September 3, 1783. Four years later, the United States Constitution was signed on September 17. Help students calculate how many years ago each of these key events took place.

AND, September is also—

☆ **Be Kind to Editors and Writers Month**

☆ **Children's Good Manners Month**

☆ **National Mushroom Month**

☆ **National Rice Month**

SEPTEMBER by the WEEK

WEEK 1 National Veterinary Week

Present math projects related to animals and animal health during this week.

⊚ **Two-legs, four legs, six legs, or more:**
   Which sick creatures come to my door?
   Create nontraditional problems about animal legs you might see in a vet's waiting room. Have students guess and test or draw pictures to find sensible solutions. For example: In her waiting room, Dr. Vette saw 18 legs, not counting people. The legs were on 5 different animals. What could they have been? (Sample answer: 1 cat, 1 dog, 1 parrot, 1 rabbit, 1 goat.) Have children create, exchange, and solve each other's problems.

⊚ **Birth Data:** One important job veterinarians do is to examine newborn animal babies. Different kinds of animals give birth to (or hatch) different numbers of babies at once. Have students find the average number of baby animals normally born to different kinds of animal parents. Help them present the data in a table or chart. Use the findings in compare-and-contrast problems.

AND, the first week in September is also—

☆ **Brazil Independence Week**
☆ **Child Injury Prevention Week**

WEEK 2 Substitute Teacher Appreciation Week

Invite children to substitute for you to do some mathematical teacher chores.

⊚ Ask volunteers to take attendance by marking absences on a table or chart.

⊚ Substitute teachers probably have to take milk or lunch counts. Challenge children to devise ways to gather and record this information clearly and accurately. Have them present the data to the office or lunchroom.

AND, the second week in September is also—

☆ **National 5-a-Day Week** (refers to servings of fruits and veggies)

10

WEEK 3 ⟩ Balance Awareness Week

This event is intended to build public awareness of the importance of the body's internal systems of balance. Why not build awareness of balance scales?

⚙ **To Scale:** Provide (or help children make) simple balance scales. Let students use them to compare various objects by weight. Discuss differences between scales that show units of measure (like bathroom scales or postage scales) and balance scales that are used to compare or approximate the weights of items.

⚙ **On Balance:** Try simple balance experiments. Use the scales children have already constructed. Have them create and record "equations" that balance, such as 3 crayons = 1 chalk eraser, or 1 10-rod = 4 snap cubes.

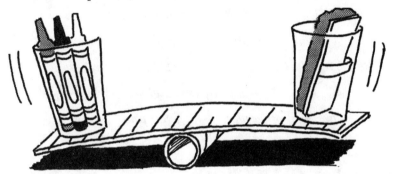

AND, the third week in September is also—

☆ **Fall Hat Week**

☆ **National School Internet Safety Week**

WEEK 4 ⟩ National Imperfection Week

This commemorates something everyone can appreciate! Help students see that mistakes aren't always bad—in fact, they can be excellent learning tools. (If your students are perfect, skip these activities.)

⚙ **Perfecting Estimates:** Do lots of estimation activities this week: How many beads in a jar? How many coins in a change purse? How many words in a paragraph? Before you present estimation challenges to students, determine an exact count yourself. Then use guesses that are too great or too small to model how students can use their first guess to make a better second guess.

⚙ **Almost-Perfect Circles:** Let children use a compass to draw some (nearly) perfect circles. They need not know all the math concepts of circles to get hands-on experience with radii, diameters, area, and circumference. Have them vary the size of the radius to make different circles and to create interesting math art designs.

AND, the fourth week in September is also—

☆ **Deaf Awareness Week**

☆ **National Dog Week**

September by the Day

SEPTEMBER 1 | Investigate Phone Numbers

Emma M. Nutt Day honors the first woman telephone operator. Nutt (1849–1926) began her job in Boston on this day in 1878 and worked until she retired in 1911. Have children investigate patterns they can find in telephone numbers. Provide a list of class phone numbers or some numbers from a local directory. Ask:

- ☉ *Are any palindromes (read the same backward and forward)?*
- ☉ *Do any have all odd (or even) digits?*
- ☉ *Which have digits in ascending (or descending) order?*
- ☉ *Which have repeated digits?*
- ☉ *Which have all different digits?*
- ☉ *What other patterns can you find?*

SEPTEMBER 2 | Coin Check

It's the anniversary of the U.S. Treasury Department. On this day in 1789, Congress set up the Treasury Department to oversee all financial functions, such as collecting taxes, manufacturing coins and bills, and regulating banks. Have children examine American coins to find common features—date, motto, portrait of a historical figure. Extend to include bills and/or foreign coins. Invite children to design their own original coins that incorporate the key features.

SEPTEMBER 3 | What's in a Newspaper?

On this day in 1833 publisher Benjamin Day introduced the *New York Sun*, America's first successful penny newspaper. Readers liked its low price, its human-interest stories, and the eager "newsies" who hawked it on street corners. The nation's first newsie was 10-year-old Barney Flaherty. Examine today's newspapers in various ways:

- ☉ *How much does an issue cost?*
- ☉ *How many pages (sections) does it have?*
- ☉ *How many columns are on a page? Is every page the same?*
- ☉ *Are there more stories, pictures, or ads?*
- ☉ *Are they printed in color, in black-and-white, or both?*

Help students find out how much money newsies can earn selling or delivering papers in your area. Or find out how much money the class can earn by collecting and recycling newspapers.

SEPTEMBER 4 | Ceiling Scrapers

Today is the birthday of Daniel Burnham (1846–1912), American architect and city planner. He designed the first of many tall buildings we've come to call skyscrapers. Have student groups construct their own skyscrapers in the classroom, using any available materials: snap cubes, blocks, cardboard tubes, paper rolls, and so on. Establish rules for construction, such as the tower must be free-standing, or its base must be at least one square foot. Allow ample time for young architects to work, then have them measure the height of their towers to the nearest half-inch or centimeter. Present the data as a class list.

SEPTEMBER 5 | Time Enough?

Be Late for Something Day was invented by the Procrastinator's Club of America. This group believes it's good to be late sometimes, just to avoid stress. Today, focus on story problems that involve elapsed time. For example, try this:

A movie lasts 95 minutes. It starts at 2:00. When will it end? When should your dad leave to come get you so he won't be late?

Create similar problems, and encourage children to make up their own. Discuss the idea of leaving a little extra time "just in case." Also help students work backward to determine suitable times. For instance:

It takes 25 minutes to get to the dentist's office. What time should you leave to make your 4:45 appointment on time?

SEPTEMBER 6 | TV Ratios

Happy Swaziland Independence Day! In 1968 this African agricultural nation gained its independence from Britain. The *World Almanac* says that, on average, there is one television set for every 50 Swazi people. Using the same ratio as in Swaziland, about how many television sets would you need for your school? Help students understand this simple ratio concept by creating and extending a table:

50 people	100 people	150 people	200 people
1 television	2 televisions	3 televisions	?

SEPTEMBER 7 | The Pulse of a Class

Happy Birthday to Michael DeBakey (b. 1908), heart surgeon. Dr. DeBakey gained worldwide fame by perfecting an artificial heart pump for people with seriously damaged hearts. To honor his achievement, talk about the role of the heart as a muscle that pumps blood throughout the body.

Help students learn to find their own pulse rates.

⊚ *Show how to find a carotid pulse (on the side of the neck), the pulse in the inner wrist (above the thumb), or the heartbeat itself on the left side of the chest.*

⊚ *Students count beats for 15 seconds and multiply that number by 4, or count for 30 seconds and double the number, to estimate their pulse rate for 1 minute.*

Extend by having students take their pulses after energetic activity, during a quiet moment, after lunch, and so on, to see if they can make any generalizations about pulse patterns. Have them record and display their findings in a table.

SEPTEMBER 9 | Date Doubles

Today, the number of the day (9) is the same as the number of the month (9). Have students figure out how many such days there are in any given year. (12). Have children work in pairs to figure out if any special events occur on any of this year's "date doubles." For example, 1/1 (January 1) is New Year's Day, and 2/2 (February 2) is Groundhog Day. Does anyone you know have a birthday on a date double?

SEPTEMBER 10 | A Stitch in Time...

It's "Sew Be It!" Day, honoring the anniversary of the patent on the sewing machine in 1846. A stitch in time can hold together different parts of your math program. Students can—

⊚ *Sew a simple beanbag to use when playing math games.*

⊚ *Stitch a slipcase that can hold math flash cards.*

⊚ *Embroider a class sampler with math facts.*

⊚ *Start work on a class quilt to reflect a topic of your choice.*

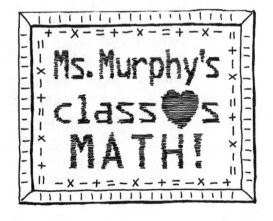

14

SEPTEMBER 11 | Starting a Business

Today is "I Want to Start My Own Business" Day. Help students imagine setting up a simple business of their own. Guide them with questions like these:

- ☺ *What would your business be? Who would your customers be?*
- ☺ *How would you make money? What expenses would you have?*
- ☺ *How many workers would you need to help you?*

Provide students with imaginary "seed money," say $200, and have them plan how best to spend it to get their business up and running.

SEPTEMBER 12 | Starry Arrays

It's Defenders Day. Each year on this day, history fans in Baltimore, Maryland, re-enact the 1814 bombardment of Fort McHenry. That event inspired Francis Scott Key to compose "The Star-Spangled Banner." Sing the song with your class. Then provide star stickers and dark blue paper. Invite children to plan different arrays or patterns for displaying the changing numbers of stars that have appeared on our flag over time: 13, 15, 20, 48, 49, and 50. Display the designs and invite students to explain the patterns they see.

SEPTEMBER 13 | Balancing Time

In India on this day in 1995, Amresh Kumar Jha began to balance on one foot. He lifted one foot in the air, and without ever resting it on anything else, including his other leg, he managed to keep his balance for 71 hours and 40 minutes! If you could repeat his one-footed feat, starting now, what day and at what time would you put your other foot back down?

SEPTEMBER 14 | Multicultural Math Games

It's International Cross-Cultural Day. People around the world use this event to celebrate the diversity that gives each nation its distinctive heritage and culture. In America, where so many cultures come together, this is a perfect day to play multicultural math games. Two essential resources are *The Multicultural Game Book* by Louise Orlando (Scholastic Professional Books) and *Multicultural Mathematics Materials* by Marina C. Krause (NCTM). Some age-appropriate games include *Senet, Mancala,* and *Wari* from Africa; *Ko-no, Fan Tan, Nim,* and *Tangrams* from Asia; *Mora* and *Fox and Geese* from Europe; and *Papago, Patolli,* and *the Bowl Game* from the Americas. Or invite parents who grew up in other cultures to demonstrate math strategy games they played as children.

SEPTEMBER 15 | Math Mysteries

It's the birthday of Agatha Christie (1890–1976). This renowned British author of mysteries gave us the inimitable sleuths Miss Marple and Hercule Poirot. Pose some math mysteries for students to solve today. For example:

⊚ *What year in the twentieth century reads the same upside down and right-side up?* (1961)

⊚ *What years in the twentieth century have digits that add up to 20?* (1919, 1928, 1937, 1946, 1955, 1964, 1973, 1982, 1991)

⊚ *At what times during a school day do the clock hands form a straight line?* (8:11 A.M., 9:16 A.M., 10:21 A.M., 11: 27 A.M., 12:33 P.M., 1:38 P.M., 2:44 P.M.)

SEPTEMBER 16 | Time for Seattle

Believe it or not, today is "Stay Away From Seattle!" Day. Seattle has become such a popular place to visit and live that locals came up with this idea to give others a break from thinking about going there. But why miss the fun in the Emerald City? Ask:

⊚ *What time is it in Seattle when it's noon where you live?*

⊚ *How far is it from where you live to Seattle?*

⊚ *How many more (or fewer) people live in Seattle than where you live?*

SEPTEMBER 17 | Estimate School Time

Today is National Student Day. Celebrate students' participation in the learning process by helping them estimate how many days of their lives they have spent in school. Use approximate figures, such as 180 days in a school year. Extend by having them estimate how many hours they have spent in school so far this year.

SEPTEMBER 18 | Pendulum Bowling

Today's the birthday of Jean Bernard Léon Foucault (1819–1868), the French scientist whose pendulum proved that the earth rotates. Honor his experiment by doing pendulum bowling. Form a pendulum by tying a beanbag to a string and hanging it from a horizontal bar or tree branch. Make it long enough to just miss the floor or ground. Set up ten plastic bottles as bowling pins, and have children use the pendulum to "bowl." Invent rules and keep score. Have kids observe and describe the path of the pendulum as it swings. You might also have children try this activity at home with their families.

SEPTEMBER 21 | Double Crossings

On this day in 1961, Antonio Abertondo became the first person to swim across the English Channel and back, nonstop! This remarkable and soggy round-trip took him 24 hours and 25 minutes. To date, there have been 22 successful double crossings. The current world record for this round-trip swim, set in 1987 by New Zealander Philip Rush, is 16 hours and 10 minutes. By how much did Rush beat Abertondo's time? (8 hours 15 minutes)

SEPTEMBER 22 | Keep a Math Log

It's "Dear Diary Day," the perfect day for kids to begin keeping a math diary. Have them jot down what they learned in math class, what they want to know, or what math questions came to mind. They can also include any daily events that involve math ideas. Have them maintain their diaries for the week, the month, or the year!

SEPTEMBER 23 | Neptunian Numbers

On this day in 1846, astronomers first saw Neptune. Gather math facts about this planet, such as its order and distance from the Sun (8th planet, about 2,797,000,000 miles), its diameter (about 31,000 miles), and the time it takes to orbit the Sun (164.8 years). They can compare these figures with the analogous ones for Earth.

SEPTEMBER 24 | Muppet Math

Happy Birthday, Jim Henson (1936–1990), creator of the puppet characters known as Muppets. Henson introduced the first Muppets in 1954 on a children's television show in Washington, D.C. *Sesame Street* first aired in 1969. Have children figure out how long ago each event took place. Then have them list some Muppet characters. Have a class vote on which Muppet is the favorite, the silliest, the wisest, the one you'd most like to have as your friend, and so on. Tally the votes and present the results in a table or graph.

SEPTEMBER 25 | Doubles and Pairs

On this day in 1882, major league ball clubs from Providence, Rhode Island and Worcester, Massachusetts played professional baseball's very first "doubleheader." Brainstorm with the class for things they know that come in doubles, such as socks, eyes, bicycle wheels, slices of bread for a sandwich, and so on. Use the list to count by twos or to explore the concept of symmetry.

SEPTEMBER 26 | Eating Fractions

Happy Birthday, John Chapman (1774–1845), otherwise known as "Johnny Appleseed." Try using apples to explore fraction concepts today. Get an assortment of different kinds, such as Macintosh, Delicious, Granny Smith, and so on. Compare and contrast them in terms of shape, color, size, weight, or other attributes students can judge by hands-on examination. Then cut the apples into different fractional parts: halves, fourths, sixths, and eighths. Ask children to verbalize fraction relationships, such as $\frac{1}{2} > \frac{1}{4}$. Reward them with edible apple fractions.

SEPTEMBER 28 | Chinese Math

In Taiwan today, people celebrate the birthday of Confucius (551–479 B.C.), the great Chinese teacher. Join the celebration by teaching children to write the Chinese characters for the numbers one through ten. Present simple arithmetic problems using the Chinese characters.

SEPTEMBER 29 | Plenty of Nothing

Today is Goose Day! Write the expression "goose egg" on the chalkboard and ask children what it means (zero). Brainstorm for other expressions that mean "zero," such as *zilch, nada, zip, nothing* and so on. Review what happens when you add, subtract, multiply, or divide with zero.

OCTOBER by the MONTH

What does October mean to you? Surely you can visualize colorful fall foliage, smiling jack-o'-lanterns, and festive harvest fairs. But October is also—

⊚ **National Cookie Month**
Work with students to select, prepare, and enjoy easy cookie recipes. Even if you have no oven in your school, there are numerous no-bake cookie recipes that children will enjoy. Or create a class cookie cookbook. Focus on measurements, yield, baking times, total or per-cookie costs, preparation times, and so on. Or do a cookie survey, a cookie cost comparison, or a chocolate chip count!

⊚ **Computer Learning Month**
This annual event helps people learn more about computers at home, in school, and in the working world. Use this month to set classroom goals for computer literacy and to establish plans for incorporating computers into classroom projects. Have a Share Day when kids can bring in their favorite software to demonstrate to classmates. Or sponsor Computer Comrades Day, when older kids can show younger ones how to do something new on the computer. Decide with the class on broad topics you can research on the World Wide Web. For more on Computer Learning Month, visit http://www.computerlearning.org. You might plan a fund-raiser to earn money for classroom computer equipment.

⊚ **National Dental Hygiene Month**
How much toothpaste is in a typical tube? Sure, the tube might say 3.5 ounces, but what does that really mean in terms of brushings? How could you figure this out? Plan an investigation with students to estimate about how many brushings they can get from a tube (or pump container) of toothpaste. Children can keep track at home, or do some classroom experiments to find out. (One way: Find the weight of a 1-foot strip of toothpaste; determine the number of brushings from that foot; estimate how many feet of toothpaste the tube holds to guess how many brushings in all from the tube.)

AND, October is also—

☆ **Adopt-a-Shelter-Animal Month**

☆ **The Month of the Dinosaur**

☆ **National Pizza Month**

☆ **National Popcorn Poppin' Month**

☆ **National Roller Skating Month**

☆ **National Stamp Collecting Month**

OCTOBER by the WEEK

WEEK 1 National Get Organized Week

It's the ideal time for activities that focus on sorting, classifying, and arranging.

- **Gizmo Sort:** How might you sort a handful of small objects? (Think of hardware items, art supplies, buttons, coins, or odds and ends you might find in a drawer or toy chest.) Try it and find out.

- **ID Ideas:** What numbers identify a person? Brainstorm a list of them. Invite students to compile a number ID booklet that includes numerical organizers such as birthday, phone number, address, ZIP code, and so on.

- **Schedules:** Create a class schedule. Work together to design an easy-to-read poster of what to do when. Make it interactive and adjustable. Children can make copies of their own, or they can contribute to the group effort.

AND, the first week in October is also—

- ☆ **Newspaper Week in Japan**
- ☆ **No Salt Week**
- ☆ **Universal Children's Week**

WEEK 2 National Metric Week

It's time to explore length, mass, and volume using units of metric measure to enhance children's metric measurement sense.

- **Meter Readers:** Provide meter sticks or metric tape measures so that students can find various lengths and distances around the classroom and the school grounds. Prepare a blank chart on which students can record what they measure.

- **Follow the Liter:** Obtain an empty liter bottle and different-sized paper cups. Have children estimate how many servings the liter would provide, based on the size of the cup. Or have them estimate how many liters it takes to fill up a sink, a bucket, or other large container. Then have them use water to find out.

- **Tell-a-Gram:** Have children estimate and then weigh assorted objects to determine their mass in grams or kilograms.

AND, the second week in October is also—

- ☆ **Fire Prevention Week**
- ☆ **National Chili Week**

20

☆ **National Spinning and Weaving Week**

☆ **Teller Appreciation Week**

WEEK 3 | National School Bus Safety Week

How much math can you find in a school bus? Use this week to find out.

◎ **Bus Data:** Do an age-appropriate mathematical analysis of a school bus. Have children quantify everything they can about the bus, such as number of seats, windows, tires, lights, capacity of gas tank, weight of the bus, size of tires, length and height of the bus, leg room, how many words or numbers appear on the outside of the bus, and so on. Compile and display the data on an informational poster or chart. Use the statistics to create school bus story problems.

◎ **Bus Logic:** Work with the class to create a Venn diagram that compares school buses with regular buses. For example, both carry passengers and have doors that a driver opens and closes. School buses are only yellow, but regular buses can be any color; cars must stop when school buses stop, but they can pass regular buses when they stop; passengers on regular buses pay a fare, but kids ride school buses for free.

AND, the third week in October is also—

☆ **National Health Education Week**

☆ **National School Lunch Week**

☆ **World Rainforest Week**

WEEK 4 | National Forest Products Week

Of the many products we use that come from forests, toothpicks are among the most inexpensive and easily available. Try some toothpick math this week.

◎ **Pick-a-Unit:** Use the toothpick as a nonstandard unit of measure. Have children find the length of classroom objects to the nearest toothpick.

◎ **Picky Puzzlers:** Present toothpick puzzlers such as this: Take away 1 toothpick to leave 2 squares. (*Hint: It's tricky.*)

AND, the fourth week in October is also—

☆ **National Save Your Back Week**

☆ **Peace, Friendship, and Goodwill Week**

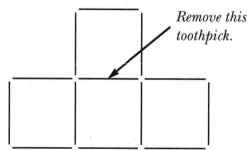

Remove this toothpick.

OCTOBER by the DAY

OCTOBER 1 | Stages of Ages

Since 1990 the United Nations has proclaimed this the International Day of Older Persons. Ask students what age they consider "old." Brainstorm to list some older people who have made a difference in your students' lives. Have children find out each individual's year of birth and use this data to calculate each person's age. Or have older children suggest age ranges to fit familiar age descriptions, such as toddler, pre-teen, teenager, young adult, middle age, and senior citizen.

OCTOBER 2 | Round the World in How Long?

In Jules Verne's famous book *Around the World in Eighty Days*, today was the day in 1872 that Phileas Fogg made a bet that he could circle the globe in 80 days or less. At that time, his was an amazing boast. Talk with children about how far it is to circumnavigate the globe (minimum distance of 22,858.8 miles), how one might do it, where, when, and why a traveler might want or need to stop, and so on. Investigate today's records for circumnavigation. (In 1994 helicopter pilot Ron Bower circled the globe in 24 days; in 1980 British pilot David Springbett made the trip in 44 hours and 6 minutes.)

OCTOBER 4 | 3, 2, 1—Liftoff!

On this date in 1957, the Space Age began when Russian scientists launched the satellite Sputnik into orbit. It weighed 184 pounds and transmitted radio signals back to Earth for 21 days. Have students figure out the date Sputnik's radio broadcasts ended. Interested students can find out more about records and achievements in the early days of the Space Race and chart or graph the information.

OCTOBER 5 | Radio Rankings

Back in 1921, baseball's World Series was broadcast over the radio for the first time ever. In that historic game, the New York Yankees beat the New York Giants 3–0. Commemorate the day by listing some radio stations that broadcast in your area. Give station call letters and numerical location on the radio dial, and have children organize them in order—from lowest to highest.

OCTOBER 6   *Ein, Zwei, Drei!*

National German-American Day was established in 1987 to recognize the many contributions German Americans have made to our nation. Your class can celebrate by learning how to count to ten in German: ein, zwei, drie, vier, fünf, sechs, sieben, acht, neun, zehn. Discuss which of the German words sound most like English words for the same numbers.

OCTOBER 7   **Miles of Aisles**

America's largest public library opened on this day in 1991. The Harold Washington Library Center in Chicago has almost 71 miles of bookshelves! Work as a class to estimate the number of miles (or kilometers) of bookshelves in your school library.

OCTOBER 8   **Stock Talk**

On this day in 1896, the Dow Jones Industrial Average (DJIA) began daily reports of stock market activity. Since then, the Dow has been a gauge for investors. To honor this day, write the value of yesterday's DJIA on the board. Tell children that the stock market is a place where investors can buy and sell shares of businesses, thus becoming part owners. If a company does well, the shareholders make money; if a company does poorly, its shareholders lose money. The DJIA is a measure that shows how well or poorly stocks are doing. This number changes constantly. Have children predict whether the Dow will rise or fall in value today. After the market closes (4 P.M. EST), record the final number and check class predictions. Do basic financial literacy activities by tracking the Dow for a few weeks or by following a stock children will recognize, such as Disney, McDonald's, or Microsoft.

OCTOBER 9   **How Long Is a Minute?**

On this day in 1806, African-American scientist and mathematician Benjamin Banneker (b. 1736) died. One of Banneker's most amazing accomplishments was the hand-carving of a wooden clock that worked—yet he'd never seen a clock before! Celebrate his genius by having children estimate how long a minute lasts. Have them close their eyes. Give a starting signal and have them raise their hands when they think that one minute has passed. Repeat to sharpen children's time estimating skills. Challenge children to name several activities that take a minute to complete.

OCTOBER 10 | Tracking Fitness

In Japan, today is a national day of physical activity. The Japanese have celebrated this since 1966 to honor the opening of the 1964 Olympic Games in Tokyo. Have children do some physical fitness activities and keep track of times or scores. For example: *How many sit-ups can you do in one minute? How many times can you jump rope without a miss? How long can you balance on one foot?*

OCTOBER 11 | Add-a-Thon

On this day in 1887, Dorr Eugene Felt got a patent for his adding machine, the first such machine known to be accurate at all times. Nowadays, adding machines are less common than handheld calculators or the calculators built into computers, but we can still celebrate this technological advance. Have a class adding race. Have children work in groups or teams. Provide each team with a long column of one or two-digit numbers to add. At a signal, teams begin to compute. See who gets the correct total faster: students using their heads or paper and pencil, or students using adding machines or calculators.

OCTOBER 12 | Feet of Feet

On this day in 1960, Soviet Premier Nikita Krushchev went wild at a meeting of the United Nations General Assembly. In his anger, he took off his shoe and pounded it on his table! Have students remove their shoes and measure the length of their feet. (Students should measure both feet since they often differ in length.) How many feet of feet does each child have? How many feet of feet are in your entire class (counting you)?

OCTOBER 14 | Try Something Hard

It's National Train Your Brain Day! The sponsors of this event say we use but a small portion of our full brain power, so they've set aside this day as a time to learn something new and stretch our mental frontiers. Present a new math fact to memorize, an especially hard spelling word to learn, or a new way of thinking. For instance, you might present the fact 12 x 12 = 144, or demonstrate the estimation techniques of compatible numbers, front-end estimation, or flexible rounding. Or you might present the subtraction method of division. The sky's the limit!

OCTOBER 15 | Smile Lengths

Well, all you grumblers out there, today is National Grouch Day! The sponsors believe that even grouches deserve to be honored. So, to balance the ill humor that's sure to surface today, invite children to measure their brightest smiles. Use string to measure the widest smile and find its length to the nearest quarter inch or centimeter. For contrast, children can measure the scrunchiest frown to the nearest quarter inch or centimeter. Or they can display the sourest pusses they can make.

OCTOBER 16 | Look Up Math Words

Happy Dictionary Day! This event honors the birth of Noah Webster (1758–1843), who compiled one of the earliest dictionaries of the English language. Take this opportunity to challenge children to spell some tricky math words, such as *quotient, multiplication, parallelogram,* or *rhombus.* Or write some unknown math terms on the board, such as *subtrahend, minuend,* or *circumference,* and challenge children to use a dictionary to find out what they mean.

OCTOBER 18 | Rate the States

Today is Alaska Day, the anniversary of the transfer of that territory from Russia to the United States in 1867. Alaska is the largest state in the Union, but it does not rank #1 in every category. Help children prepare a chart that compares your state with Alaska in terms of area, population, number of representatives, miles of highway, and other such indicators. This data is available in any almanac. If you live in Alaska, compare Alaska with Delaware, the state with the smallest area.

OCTOBER 19 | Climb Every Mountain!

Happy Birthday to Annie Smith Peck (1850–1935). In 1908 she became the first person to climb the north peak of Mount Huascaran in Peru, which was the highest altitude ever reached in the Western Hemisphere at that time. Three years later she became the first person to climb Mount Coropuna, also in Peru—and she was sixty-one years old at the time! Have children find out the height of the tallest mountain in each continent and make a table or graph that compares them. Or have children rank the top seven mountains in your state by height.

OCTOBER 20 | Just Skip It!

In 1991 in Wimberley, Texas, someone named Jerdone tossed a stone in such a way that it skipped 38 times across water. How great a distance could children cover if they made 38 skips in a row (across land, of course!)? First guess, then try it.

OCTOBER 21 | Lightbulb!

In 1879 Thomas Edison perfected his first working incandescent bulb at his lab in Menlo Park, New Jersey. The bulb was able to burn for 13 hours. At that rate, about how many of those early bulbs would it take to light your classroom for one school week?

OCTOBER 23 | Thai Tastes

In Thailand it's Chulalongkorn Day, which recalls the death of King Chulalongkorn the Great (1853–1910), who reigned for forty-two years. He was the real-life son of King Mongkut, whose life was the basis for the famous musical *The King and I*. Cassava, the plant from which tapioca comes, is a major Thai crop. Honor Chulalongkorn Day by making and enjoying some tapioca pudding. Add some coconut, another important Thai crop, for a more authentic Thai taste.

OCTOBER 24 | Flag Fractions

Since 1948 this has been United Nations Day, the anniversary of the founding of the multinational organization that works for world peace. Have children look at pictures of the flags of many nations to find ones that show fractional parts. For instance, the flag of France is divided into thirds, as are the flags of Armenia, Benin, and Chad. The flags of the Dominican Republic, Jamaica, and Panama are divided into fourths. Help children find flags divided into halves, as well as ones that do not show equivalent fractional parts, such as the flags of Nepal or Pakistan. Older children can organize this information into a table or graph.

OCTOBER 25 | Sour Power

An Ann Arbor man has developed Sourest Day as a way to emphasize the balance of things in nature. Perhaps he objected to Sweetest Day (October 17). Take time this day to examine lemons. Have groups study a lemon's weight, length, circumference, and the amount of juice it will yield when squeezed. You can use litmus paper to test the acidity of the lemons and to compare whether all lemons students investigate have the same degree of acidity. Celebrate by making fresh lemonade!

OCTOBER 26 | Albany to Buffalo

The Erie Canal was opened on this day in 1825, providing a major waterway that connected Lake Erie to the Hudson River. Show it on a United States map. The Erie Canal was the nation's first major artificially built waterway. The project took eight years and cost over $7 million. Have children find the total length of the original Erie Canal (363 miles) and figure out where they might end up if a canal of similar length were built from your community in any direction. Sing the song "Erie Canal," which mentions the mules that walked along the towpaths hauling heavy barges.

OCTOBER 27 | Shopping Spree

On this day in 1858, R. H. Macy & Company opened its first store. Although the store eventually became part of the gigantic Macy's empire known around the world, on that day the store took in $1,106. Today, have a pretend shopping spree. Gather some general merchandise catalogs that pairs or groups of children can use to "spend" an imaginary $1,106 on whatever they want. Allow a tax-free spree. Have children estimate and use calculators to check their totals.

OCTOBER 28 | Statue Stats

On this day in 1886, the Statue of Liberty, one of the most famous of all American symbols, was dedicated on Bedloe's Island (now called Liberty Island) in New York Harbor. A gift of the French people, the statue was designed and built by sculptor Frédéric Auguste Bartholdi (1834–1904) with engineering help from Gustave Eiffel (1832–1923). Have children find statistics about the great statue. Help them make a scale drawing of Lady Liberty, or use benchmarks to get a sense of the statue's size by comparing its different measurements to familiar objects or distances.

OCTOBER 30 | Hoop Scores

Today is National Basketball Coaches Day. This event is dedicated to the many coaches around the country who help young people learn to play this internationally popular game. Tell students that in basketball today, a player can earn 1 point for a free throw, 2 points for a standard field goal, and 3 points for an extra-long field goal. Challenge children to come up with at least 5 different ways that a basketball player could accrue 30 points. (Sample: 10 field goals, 3 3-point shots, 1 free throw) Extend by having children try this activity using different point totals.

November by the Month

November brings shorter days, chillier winds, and thoughts of holidays and family gatherings soon to come. But November also brings—

🌀 **Aviation History Month**

Discuss the early flight experiments that the Montgolfier brothers of France conducted during this month. Their curiosity and research led to the invention of the hot air balloon and spurred the modern science of aviation. Honor Aviation History Month by using the hot air balloon motif on an interactive bulletin board of math facts. Or conduct gravity-defying activities, such as paper airplane flight contests, parachute drops, and other investigations that involve keeping objects off the ground for as long as possible. Measure, time, or quantify the results, and present them in graphs or charts. You might also have children gather statistics about other early aviation firsts, which they can present in any suitable format.

🌀 **International Creative Child and Adult Month**

This celebration invites us to recognize everyday creativity along with the unique triumphs of the gifted and talented. It's a great time to highlight math art activities that tap children's spatial creativity. For instance, they can create designs based on repeated geometric shapes. They can make grid paper mosaics (akin to the use of pixels in computer graphics) or use perpendicular and parallel lines to create abstract images. Younger children might invent cartoonlike figures based on the numerals 0–9 or use pattern blocks to create desktop designs. This month invites adult creativity also; don't forget to take part.

🌀 **International Drum Month**

Recognizing, replicating, and extending patterns is a big math idea. This month, excite auditory and musical learners by celebrating International Drum Month with pattern making. Children can make their own drums or use real rhythm instruments or found objects to produce clear rhythmic patterns. Take turns in a call-and-response format, where different leaders offer a rhythmic pattern for others to play back. Start with simple patterns and move to more complex ones as children become more adept. Extend by creating a code system for notating rhythmic patterns.

AND, November is also—

☆ **National Diabetes Month**

☆ **National Fragrance Month**

☆ **Peanut Butter Lover's Month**

NOVEMBER by the WEEK

WEEK 1 — National Chemistry Week

Present math projects related to chemistry anytime this week.

- **Grow Crystals:** Have children cut up sponges into 1-inch cubes. Put some in a pie tin. Mix: $\frac{1}{2}$ cup water; $\frac{1}{2}$ cup salt; $\frac{1}{2}$ cup blueing; and 2 tablespoons ammonia. Soak the sponge cubes with the mixture. Set the pie tin near a window. Have children observe every two hours as crystals start to form. After three days add a small amount of water to prolong the growth of the crystals.

- **Temperature Tests:** Fill three jars with water, each of a different temperature. Record the temperature of each jar. Then add 1 tablespoon of salt to each jar and see how long it takes for all the salt grains to dissolve. Children should observe that the warmer the water, the faster the salt will dissolve.

AND, the first week in November is also—

☆ **National Fig Week**

☆ **World Communication Week**

WEEK 2 — National Split Pea Soup Week

Let this lovely legume lead the list this week.

- **Reci-Peas:** Find a simple recipe for split pea soup (with or without meat), and prepare it with your students. For fun, add some alphabet noodles! Have a class lunch of soup, bread, fruit, and milk for a healthy, low-cost meal.

- **Peas, Please:** Use split peas for estimation and measurement activities:

    - *How many split peas can you hold in your hand?*
    - *How much does a cup of split peas weigh?*
    - *Which is heavier: a cup of split peas or a cup of water?*
    - *How long is a row of 50 split peas?*

AND, the second week in November is also—

☆ **Operating Room Nurse Week**

☆ **Pursuit of Happiness Week**

WEEK 3 | National Geography Awareness Week

Math and maps naturally go together, and this is the week to make the connections. Scales help children use a given map scale to estimate distances. They can use standard or nonstandard measures to determine distance between points.

- ◎ **Mapmaking:** Provide grid paper and measuring tools to help children create a map to scale. They can map some or all of the classroom, the playground, the library, or another spot around school; or they can map a regulation sports playing field, such as a baseball diamond, football field, bowling lane, or basketball court. Help them establish a simple scale, such as 1 box = 1 foot.

- ◎ **Mathiverse Map:** Invite children to create a map of an imaginary place called Mathiverse. Mathiverse can have sites such as Circle Lake, Triangle Mountain, or Parallel Park, as well as towns like Decimal Point or Numberville.

AND, the third week in November is also—
- ☆ **American Education Week**
- ☆ **National Children's Book Week**

WEEK 4 | National Game and Puzzle Week

Present math puzzles and play math games to celebrate this event.

- ◎ **Way to Play!:** Encourage children to play commercially available logic games, such as chess, *Go, Othello, Battleship, Triominoes, Mastermind,* or *Mancala.* Or consult *Quick-and-Easy Learning Games: Math* by Marcia K. Miller, or *Mega-Fun Math Games* by Dr. Michael Schiro (both available from Scholastic Professional Books) for scores of easy-to-play math games.

- ◎ **Coin Puzzles:** Provide play money children can use to act out or model simple coin problems. For example: I have 5 coins, but no nickels. The coins total 47¢. What coins do I have? (1 quarter, 2 dimes, 2 pennies)

AND, the fourth week in November is also—
- ☆ **National Adoption Week**
- ☆ **National Family Caregivers Week**

NOVEMBER by the DAY

NOVEMBER 1 \ Math and Literature

National Author's Day has been celebrated since 1929. Your class can celebrate this day by focusing on authors of math stories. Read some books aloud, or have children form small groups to read, share, and discuss all-time favorites, such as *The 329th Friend* by Marjorie Weinman Sharmat, *The Philharmonic Gets Dressed* by Karla Kuskin, *The Goat in the Rug* by Charles L. Blood and Martin Link, *How Big Is a Foot?* by Rolf Myller, *The Doorbell Rang* by Pat Hutchins, *Grandfather Tang's Story* by Ann Tompert, *Sea Squares* by Joy N. Hulme, and *King Kaid of India* (traditional), to name but a few. Create a math authors' book display.

NOVEMBER 3 \ Tasty Combinations

It's Sandwich Day, to honor the birthday of John Montague (1718–1792), Fourth Earl of Sandwich. In 1762 he supposedly invented the notion of holding and eating a piece of meat between slices of bread, thus opening up a new taste treat for all the world to enjoy. Kids will eat up math problems about sandwiches. Present a few:

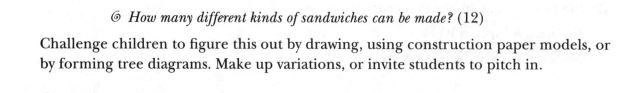

- ☺ *You have 3 kinds of bread: white, rye, and pita.*

- ☺ *You have 2 kinds of meat: turkey and roast beef.*

- ☺ *You can add either lettuce or tomato, but not both.*

- ☺ *How many different kinds of sandwiches can be made?* (12)

Challenge children to figure this out by drawing, using construction paper models, or by forming tree diagrams. Make up variations, or invite students to pitch in.

NOVEMBER 4 \ Egyptian Math

On this day in 1922, British archaeologists found the tomb of Pharaoh Tutankhamen, the child-king who ruled Egypt from the age of 9 to 19. King Tut's tomb was discovered over 3,000 years after the king died. Observe this day by showing children how to write numbers in Egyptian hieroglyphics. Note that the symbol for ones, tens, and hundreds is repeated as often as necessary to build a number. So, 368 is shown with 3 hundreds hieroglyphs, 6 tens hieroglyphs, and 8 ones hieroglyphs. The Egyptians grouped the hieroglyphs to fit a given space, as shown below.

1, 2, 3,...9	10, 20, 30,...90	100, 200, 300,...900
I, II, III,... IIIIIIIII	∩, ∩∩, ∩∩∩, ...∩∩∩∩∩∩∩∩∩	9, 99, 999, ...999999999

NOVEMBER 6 | Basketball Facts

Happy Birthday to James Naismith (1861–1939), the man who invented basketball. Honor Naismith by playing a number facts game using beanbags and a trash can. Divide the class into two or more teams. Each team member in turn tosses a beanbag at the basket. If it goes in, that team get 2 points and poses a number fact to the opposing team. If the opposing team answers correctly, they get 1 point and the chance to shoot. If the team answers incorrectly, the first team gets 1 point and shoots again. Vary the rules as you see fit.

NOVEMBER 7 | What's in a Name?

Today is National Notary Public Day. Tell students that a notary public is a person who is authorized by law to witness and certify official signatures on documents or legal papers. Discuss the significance of a legal signature. Then have children write their own official signature and do an analysis of it in terms of number of vowels and consonants. Have them make a bar graph that compares these numbers. Display the graphs and challenge children to look for someone whose signature has properties similar to their own.

NOVEMBER 8 | Comet Watch

Happy Birthday to Edmund Halley (1656–1742), the astronomer and mathematician who first observed the Great Comet of 1682, which was eventually given his name. He predicted that the comet would reappear in 1758—and it did. Tell students that Halley's Comet is next expected to appear in the year 2061. Have them figure out how many years away this is and how old they will be in that year.

NOVEMBER 9 | Blackout Math

On this day in 1965, over 30 million people in the northeastern United States and parts of Canada experienced the greatest electrical blackout in history. The power in New York City went out at 5:27 P.M., and stayed out for about $13\frac{1}{2}$ hours! Have students estimate when the power came back on (about 7 A.M., the next morning).

NOVEMBER 11 \ Read n' Write Math

It's National Young Reader's Day. This is the perfect day to read aloud math stories children have created. You might suggest story topics to children, math ideas to include, or characters to develop. If children write math story problems, they can read them aloud in small groups for classmates to solve.

NOVEMBER 12 \ National Park Math

Dramatic red sandstone arches and other striking products of natural erosion led Congress, on this day in 1929, to set aside more than 73,000 acres of land near Moab, Utah, as Arches National Monument. In 1971 Arches became a National Park. Have children use modeling clay to create the longest freestanding arch they can. Have them measure the distance between the bases of their arches and chart or graph the data. Older children can find Arches on a map of Utah, and estimate about how far it is from your community by car.

NOVEMBER 13 \ Treasure Maps

Happy Birthday to Robert Louis Stevenson (1850–1894), author of such adventure classics as *Treasure Island, Kidnapped,* and *The Strange Case of Dr. Jekyll and Mr. Hyde.* Honor this writer by inviting children to create their own treasure maps. They can "bury" an imaginary treasure somewhere in the classroom or on the school grounds. Then they can make a simple map and provide clues to its location, such as "Go 5 steps north" or "Turn left at the hydrant." Pairs can follow each other's maps.

NOVEMBER 14 \ Circulation Estimation

On this day in 1666, diarist Samuel Pepys described an astonishing new medical procedure: blood transfusion. Nowadays, blood transfusions are common medical practice. Have children guess the amount of blood that travels through the human body. Tell them that average adult humans have $10\frac{1}{2}$ pints of blood coursing through their veins. Then use a measuring cup and a pitcher or bowl to model how much liquid this is.

NOVEMBER 15 \ Odds and Evens

On this day in Japan, families celebrate *Shichi-go-san,* or the "Seven-Five-Three" children's festival. Parents of 3-year-old boys or girls, 5-year-old boys, and 7-year-old girls dress their children in their best traditional garments and go to a local shrine, where the children receive blessings of good health and future success. The Japanese believe that odd numbers are lucky. Review odd and even numbers. Challenge children to make generalizations about the outcomes of operations with odd and even numbers. For instance: *What happens when you add two odd numbers? Two even numbers? One of each? What about when you multiply?* Invite groups to present their findings and explain their reasoning.

NOVEMBER 16 | More Than One Way

The United Nations has proclaimed this the International Day for Tolerance. The members hope to remind people of the importance of respecting other individuals or nations whose ideas or customs differ from their own. Try an exercise to encourage tolerance—for different ways of expressing a mathematical quantity. Challenge children to come up with as many different ways as possible to express 16, such as:

$$16 = 10 + 6$$
$$= 8 \times 2$$
$$= 4^2$$
$$= 20 - 4$$
$$= XVI$$

NOVEMBER 17 | Mathematical Mystery

Happy Birthday to August Möbius (1790–1868), the German teacher whose name was given to an unusual mathematical property he described. The Möbius strip is a figure with only one side! Children can make a Möbius strip to explore this puzzling idea for themselves. Here's how: Take a strip of paper at least 15 inches long and about 1 inch wide. Bring the ends together as if to make a loop, but before attaching the ends, give one side a twist and then attach. The resulting figure is the mystifying Möbius strip. Have children draw a continuous crayon line along the Möbius strip as far as they can go without ever lifting up the crayon. They will find that they end up where they began, proving that the Möbius strip has only one side.

NOVEMBER 18 | Mouse Math

On this day in 1928, an international star was born. He was featured in the world's first talking animated cartoon, *Steamboat Willie*, which opened at the Colony Theatre in New York City. The character was a funny rodent with four fingers on each gloved hand. His name: Mickey Mouse! Have children figure out how old Mickey would be today and when he'll be a "mouse-entenarian" (100 years old).

NOVEMBER 19 \ From Bad to Good

Weary of the cheery "Have a nice day"? If so, then this is the day you've been waiting for: It's "Have a Bad Day" Day! The idea of this tongue-in-cheek event is to balance out all that sweetness with a little tang! You can join the fun by presenting students with a page of math facts all of which are wrong. Challenge them to correct each mistake, turning the paper from a bad one to a good one.

NOVEMBER 20 \ Postage Math

On or about this day, the York International Postcard Fair is held. Interested visitors gather to see, buy, sell, or trade postcards. Present this postal challenge to your class: Suppose you took a class trip somewhere, and everyone in the class decided to mail a postcard back home. How much would it cost if everyone sent a card, including the teacher? Obtain current postage rates from any post office. Extend the challenge by figuring the cost of sending postcards to another country such as Mexico, Korea, or Tanzania.

NOVEMBER 21 \ Greet Idea!

It's World Hello Day! People in 179 countries have taken part in this peace-loving event. To do so, people agree to greet 10 different people, one at a time. Challenge children to participate in a variation on this activity. Divide the class into groups of 3, 4, 5, or 6. Have each group figure out how many "Hellos" are said when each person in the group greets every other person.

NOVEMBER 22 \ Jungle Math

According to a famous book by Edgar Rice Burroughs, on this day in 1888 the baby who would become Tarzan of the Apes was born. To honor this classic character, do some jungle math today. For example, have children find out the heights or weights of some jungle animals, such as the gorilla, giraffe, elephant, and lion. Invite them to make up story problems based on the statistics they find.

NOVEMBER 23 | Horseshoe Math

On this day in 1835, Henry Burden of Troy, New York, got a patent for the first horseshoe manufacturing machine. Before this, horseshoes had to be made by hand. Have children figure out how many shoes it would take to shoe different numbers of horses: a pair (8), a team of 6 horses (24), a parade of 25 horses (100), and so on.

NOVEMBER 24 | Flight Records

Ruth Nichols (1901–1960) was an aviation pioneer many times over. She was the first woman to get an international pilot's license, to fly nonstop from New York to Miami, and to pilot a passenger airliner. On this day in 1930, she began a transcontinental flight from Long Island, New York, to Burbank, California; eight days later she arrived, beating the previous flight record by 3 hours $44\frac{1}{2}$ minutes. Nichols's flying time was 16 hours $59\frac{1}{2}$ minutes. Challenge children to figure out the previous transcontinental flight record that Nichols broke. (20 hours 44 minutes)

NOVEMBER 25 | Comparing Area

On this day in 1975, the Netherlands granted independence to one of its former colonies, Suriname. Help students locate Suriname on a map of South America. Tell them that the area of Suriname is 63,251 square miles. Provide a chart of areas of the individual states of our nation. Challenge children to determine which state is closest in size to Suriname. (Wisconsin, whose total area is 65,499 square miles)

NOVEMBER 26 | When to Give Thanks

George Washington proclaimed this day in 1789 as a day of public prayer and thanksgiving. This was the first time an American president ever proclaimed a national holiday. But it was not until Civil War days that Abraham Lincoln revived interest in the holiday and declared that it be observed annually on the fourth Thursday of November. Work together to determine the answers to these questions:

        ☺ *What is the earliest date any Thanksgiving Day can ever fall?* (11/22)

        ☺ *What is the latest possible date for any Thanksgiving Day?* (11/28)

NOVEMBER 27 | Temperature Scales

Happy Birthday, Anders Celsius (1701–1744). He was the Swedish astronomer who developed the centigrade scale for temperature. Celsius called the freezing point of water 0° and its boiling point 100°. Today, scientists around the world use the Celsius temperature scale. Have children record the temperature at various times during the day, in Fahrenheit and in Celsius, to build their number sense for temperatures. Repeat on other days, even though it's not Celsius's birthday!

NOVEMBER 28 | You Call That Speed?

America's first automobile race took place on this day in 1895. Six cars entered the race, which involved completing a 55-mile course. The winner's average speed? A blistering 7 mph! Have children use this fact to answer questions like these:

⊚ *If cars today went only that fast, about how long would it take to drive 100 miles?* (about 14 hours)

⊚ *About how long did it take the winner to complete that race?* (just under 8 hours)

⊚ *About how far can a car go in 8 hours at an average speed of 55 mph?* (440 miles)

NOVEMBER 29 | Sibling Survey

Happy Birthday, Louisa May Alcott (1832–1888), author of the classic *Little Women*. In that famous story, the March family had four girls: Meg, Jo, Beth, and Amy. Take a survey to find out how many brothers and/or sisters each child in the class has. Graph the results. Ask comparison questions based on the data.

DECEMBER by the MONTH

This month, the days grow shorter (and colder in our country), the year moves toward its end, and many cultures around the world celebrate significant festivals and holidays. But that's not all. December is—

⊚ **International Calendar Awareness Month**
Where would we be without calendars? This is the month to think about their importance in our daily lives. Explore the variety of calendars people use to get organized: individual date books, electronic organizers, write-on blank calendars, interactive classroom calendars, and so on. Recognize this event by having a calendar math scavenger hunt. Present challenges such as these, answerable with any ordinary calendar:

> ⊚ *Find an even date that falls on a Tuesday.*
> ⊚ *Find an odd date that falls on a Sunday.*
> ⊚ *Find the date of the first Thursday after the third Monday.*
> ⊚ *Find two consecutive dates that add up to 25.*
> ⊚ *Find two diagonal dates that add up to 10.*
> ⊚ *Find a date that is a multiple of 7.*
> ⊚ *Find a month with five Saturdays.*

⊚ **Safe Toys and Gifts Month**
Everyone loves to give and get gifts; this event reminds people to consider the safety of toys young children use. Prepare a poster or bulletin board with sample safe-toy ideas for children of different ages. Organize the display by age ranges: infant to 2 years, 2–4 years, 4–6 years, and older than 6. To get ideas, children can look through toy catalogs, magazines, and newspaper ads or talk with parents, pediatricians, teachers, and others who work with children.

AND, December is also—

☆ **Bingo's Birthday Month**
☆ **Universal Human Rights Month**

BUT—
In this traditionally busy month, there are no significant weekly events scheduled. Take this opportunity to enjoy the numerous daily events, or create some weeklong events of your own that reflect this time of year in your community.

December by the Day

December 1 | Sisters, Cousins, and Aunts

Gilbert and Sullivan's beloved operetta *H.M.S. Pinafore* opened in London on this day in 1879. One song from this satire describes a silly group of "sisters, cousins, and aunts" who accompany the Lord Admiral of the British Navy wherever he goes. Have children tally the total number of sisters, female cousins, and aunts they have. Make a line plot to display the data.

December 2 | Mountain Math

On this day in 1980, Mount McKinley National Park (est. February 26, 1917) and Denali National Monument (est. December 1, 1978), both in Alaska, were combined to form Denali National Park and Preserve. Mt. McKinley, at 20,320 feet, is the highest peak in the United States. Help children find the highest point in your state and compare it with McKinley. (If you live in Alaska, compare the height of McKinley with the height of Citlaltépetl, also known as Orizaba, the tallest point in Mexico at 18,406 feet.)

December 4 | Pairs

On this day in 1858, one Chester Greenwood was credited with inventing earmuffs. Have children figure out how many ears would be covered if everyone in your class wore a pair of Mr. Greenwood's earmuffs today.

December 5 | Bathtub Volume

It's Bathtub Party Day! Most people nowadays shower rather than bathe, so this event reminds us of the fun of taking bubble baths and splashing around with our favorite tub toys. Invite children to measure the inner dimensions of a bathtub (approximate length, width, and depth). Help them figure out how much water the bathtub would hold. Help younger children order bathtub data by length, height, and depth and look for patterns or relationships among these measurements.

DECEMBER 6 | Countdown 25

As of today, there are only 25 days left in this year. Challenge children to come up with as many different ways to express the quantity 25 as they can, including Roman numerals, number sentences, and so on.

DECEMBER 8 | Spinach Speculation

Happy Birthday to Elzie Segar (1894–1938). Segar created *Thimble Theater*, the cartoon world of Popeye, Olive Oyl, and related characters. Popeye grew strong whenever he ate spinach—usually from a can. Mark the event by investigating the true properties of spinach. Find out how many calories raw spinach has per cup (12) and about how many cups of raw spinach make 1 serving of cooked spinach (about 4 cups). One cup of raw spinach provides about 2 milligrams of iron. If children need about 10 milligrams of iron daily, how much spinach would they have to eat? (5 cups raw spinach, $1\frac{1}{4}$ servings cooked spinach)

DECEMBER 9 | Math in a Deep Freeze

Clarence Birdseye (1886–1956) has been called "the father of frozen foods." He invented a way to freeze fresh food without ruining it. This changed American eating and shopping habits forever. Today is the anniversary of his birth. Have children estimate how long it takes for an ice cube to melt completely. Record their estimates and then observe an ice cube as it melts in a cup. Take the temperature of the liquid when it has fully melted.

DECEMBER 10 | Book Orders

Happy Birthday to librarian Melvil Dewey (1851–1931), who invented the Dewey Decimal System, a system for classifying books used in most libraries today. Obtain an assortment of library books, each with a different Dewey Decimal call number. Have children use the numbers to put the books in order. For older children, select books with call numbers in the hundredths and thousandths.

DECEMBER 11 | Nineteenth in Order

On this day in 1816, Indiana became the nineteenth state to join the United States. Have students figure out how long Indiana has been a state. Then work together to figure out who is the nineteenth oldest student in the class.

DECEMBER 12 | The Estimate Is Right

Happy Birthday to Bob Barker (b. 1923), longtime host of the TV show *The Price Is Right*. Today, do some estimation activities according to *Price Is Right* rules: The estimate that is closest *without going over* wins. Display jars of jelly beans, cups of cotton balls, bowls of beans, and so on. Invite children to estimate how many.

DECEMBER 13 | Face Value

On this day in 1978, the U.S. Treasury issued the Susan B. Anthony silver dollar—the first American coin to honor a woman. Let children examine an Anthony silver dollar. Be sure they understand that it has the same value as a $1 bill. Display other American coins, featuring the person they honor: a Lincoln penny, a Jefferson nickel, a Roosevelt dime, a Washington quarter, and a Kennedy half-dollar. Use the portraits to present some offbeat equations for children to solve, such as:

  ☺ *2 Lincolns + 3 Jeffersons = ___ ¢ (17)*

  ☺ *2 Washingtons − 4 Roosevelts = 2 _____ (Jeffersons)*

DECEMBER 15 | Cornering Angles

Ever since 1962, today has been Bill of Rights Day. It honors the anniversary of the Bill of Rights, which expanded our Constitution in 1791. In math, the term *right angle* has nothing to do with power or privilege but with angle measure. Today, explore right angles (angles that measure exactly 90°). Challenge children to find right angles in the classroom, in letters, numerals, and in logos or design motifs.

DECEMBER 16 | Building the Pyramids

In 1986 the song "Walk Like an Egyptian" by the Bangles, was #1 on the pop music charts. It's a good day to examine the mathematical attributes of the 3-D figure known as the pyramid. Have children build pyramid models using oaktag or mini-marshmallows and toothpicks.

DECEMBER 17 | 12 Seconds, 120 Feet

On this day in 1903, brothers Wilbur and Orville Wright made the first successful powered air flight near Kitty Hawk, North Carolina. That first flight, with Orville at the controls, lasted just

42

12 seconds. The plane flew about 120 feet. Help children get a sense of both of these measures. First, have them see how high they can count, how much of the alphabet they can recite, or how much of their complete name they can write in 12 seconds. Then measure out 120 feet in the gym or school yard. Figure out how long it takes children to walk or run that distance. Older students can estimate how long 12 seconds lasts or how far 120 feet is from a given point.

DECEMBER 18 | Paper Weights?

On this day in 1796, the *Monitor* of Baltimore, Maryland, became the first Sunday newspaper published in the United States. How much does a Sunday paper weigh nowadays? Have students guess. Then collect three to five different Sunday papers, weigh them, and graph the results.

DECEMBER 20 | Land Costs

On this day in 1803, the U.S. took over vast areas of North America that had once been controlled by France. In this deal—the Louisiana Purchase—the government paid about $20 for each square mile of land. This transaction greatly increased the size of our young nation. Help children find the number of square miles in your city, county, or state. Help them estimate how much it would cost to buy that amount of land at the Louisiana Purchase rate.

DECEMBER 21 | Countdown Day

As of this day, only 10 days remain in this year. Take a few moments to count backward—from 10 to 1, from 80 to 70, from 73 to 61, from 340 to 325, and so on. Vary the task by having children count backward by tens from 100 to 0, from 543 to 443, from 2400 to 2300, and so on.

DECEMBER 23 | Pacing the Room

In 1954 the film *20,000 Leagues Under the Sea* was released on this day. The league is a unit of distance measure that equals about 3 miles, although its length has varied at different times and places. Today, have children explore other old non-standard units of measure, such as the *cubit, span, pace, fathom,* and *palm.* Measure some classroom distances using those units.

DECEMBER 26 | Boxes on Boxing Day

If you put on boxing gloves to celebrate Boxing Day, as this day is known in many nations, you'd be out for the count! This holiday has nothing to do with pugilism.

Rather, it is an occasion to give gifts to people in service positions, such as letter carriers, bus drivers, baby-sitters, and so on. In math class, take time to examine the properties of boxes: the linear dimensions of height, width, and depth and the three-dimensional concept of volume, or number of cubic units the box can hold. Have children compare the volumes of a variety of small boxes. Younger children can compare boxes in terms of the number of ones cubes they can hold.

DECEMBER 27 \ Seats on the Aisle

On this day in 1932, New York's famous Radio City Music Hall opened. It was the world's biggest movie theater, with a remarkable 5,945 seats! How does this seating capacity compare with the seating capacity of your school's auditorium? If each person in your school sat in one of the seats at Radio City Music Hall, how many seats would remain vacant?

DECEMBER 29 \ Lightbulb Math

On this day in 1848, President James Polk had the pleasure of turning on the very first gaslight in the White House. How many lightbulbs are in your classroom? Estimate, then count. Classify them: Are they incandescent, fluorescent, or halogen? Challenge older children to estimate and then determine the total number of lightbulbs in your entire school. Are there more lightbulbs than windows? Than doorknobs? Than computers?

DECEMBER 31 \ Decision Time

It's Make Up Your Mind Day! It's time to make a decision—any decision—and see it through. Tie this into math by having children use logic and number sense to help them make a decision, such as how much money to save each week toward a goal, when to leave their house to get to an appointment on time, or how much time to spend practicing the flute each day.

JANUARY by the MONTH

As the official new year begins, many people think about resolutions, diets, and what they accomplished over the past year. The month of January means many things to many people, including—

⊚ **National Be On-Purpose Month**
The founders of this event invite us to "trade confusion for clarity," so it seems like this is the right month to encourage students to verbalize their thinking as they work on math. Have them tell how they got particular answers, why they used a certain solution or computation method, or how they reasoned that their responses made sense. Emphasize that good mathematicians care about the "whys" and "hows" of both making sensible estimates and getting exact answers.

⊚ **National High-Tech Month**
This event acknowledges the bold effects technology has had on the way we live today. Take a survey to see what technological devices children rely on at home, at school, and at play. Use this month to introduce new software or high-tech hardware into your curriculum, or get your class online!

⊚ **National Soup Month**
This event celebrates this favorite dish, popular in one form or another in nearly every culture of the world. Cook an easy class soup together. Read *Stone Soup*. Encourage the school cafeteria to serve new soups this month. Take a survey to find out the favorite (or least favorite) soups in your class. Invite children to create fanciful recipes (with measurements, of course!) for pet soups, alien soups, or gross-out soups. Analyze the label on a soup can to learn the ingredients, the number of servings, the nutritional information, and so on.

AND, January is also—

☆ **National Eye Care Month**   ☆ **Oatmeal Month**

☆ **National Hot Tea Month**   ☆ **Reminiscence Month**

☆ **National Radio Month**

JANUARY by the WEEK

WEEK 1 — New Year's Resolution Week

Resolve with students to learn new math facts, formulas, or math terms this week.

⊚ **Fast Facts:** Try some fast-fact quizzes this week. Keep them short and focused on one topic, such as fact families, sums of 10, or multiplication facts through 3 x 9. Encourage children to resolve to commit these facts to memory.

⊚ **Math Mountains:** Invite children to identify a math skill or concept they find difficult. Help them focus on that "math mountain" this week so they can conquer it. Children who set goals for themselves can become highly motivated to achieve.

AND, the first week in January is also—

☆ **Celebration of Life Week**   ☆ **Lose Weight/Feel Great Week**

WEEK 2 — Universal Letter-Writing Week

Weave math into letter writing this week in one of these ways.

⊚ **Pen Pals:** Help your students become cyber-pen-pals with other children around the nation or world. Use the Internet to locate potential penpals. Two helpful sites are: PenPals 25 at http://expage.com/page/penpals25 and The DinoMail Dinosaur Club PenPal Network at www.dinosociety.org/penpal.html. Use your Web browser and search engines to locate other penpal Web sites.

⊚ **Codes:** Help children encode and decode letters written according to various codes. There are many simple codes they can follow, such as letter-number substitution codes or letter-shift codes. For instance, easy letter-number substitution codes include A = 1, B = 2, C = 3, and so on, or A = 26, B = 25, C = 24, etc. A letter-shift code might work like this: A = Z, B = Y, C = X, D = W, and so on. Here is one version of a tic-tac-toe code. Children encode their message by drawing the shape of the tic-tac-toe grid that contains only the letter in question:

Tic-Tac-Toe Code

A	B	C		J	K	L		S	T	U
D	E	F		M	N	O		V		W
G	H	I		P	Q	R		X	Y	Z

AND, the second week in January is also—

☆ **Cuckoo Dancing Week**

☆ **Wilderness Wildlife Week of Nature**

WEEK 3 | National Handwriting Analysis Week

Math and handwriting can go together in a variety of creative ways.

- **Digital Number Writing:** Children are undoubtedly familiar with the form LCD numbers take on the displays of electronic equipment, such as calculators, VCRs, and clocks. Each number is formed by illuminating two to six straight lines that appear in fixed positions within a cell. Challenge children to use a 2 x 3 region of grid paper or dot paper to try to write each digit from 0 to 9 in digital form.

- **Number Character:** Everyone's handwriting is individual, even though most of us can read the penmanship of others. This week, ask children to write numbers from 0 to 100. Older students can write decimal or fractional numbers in any suitable range. Have groups work together to analyze how people form the numbers. What features are consistent? What features are unique to certain writers? Can children identify each other's number writing?

AND, the third week in January is also—

- ☆ **Be Good to Yourself Week**
- ☆ **Healthy Weight Week**

WEEK 4 | Direct Deposit Week

Electronic fund transfer has changed some aspects of banking, as this event will attest. Students probably have little or no experience with high-tech banking, so why not step back and examine ordinary banking concepts this week?

- **Deposits and Withdrawals:** Children know the basic concepts of addition and subtraction but do not always connect those operations to the bank transactions of *depositing* and *withdrawing*. Set up a play bank where children can take turns being tellers, who handle money and authorize transactions; customers, who deposit and withdraw funds; and auditors, who verify that the transaction calculations are correct. You might create simple deposit and withdrawal forms or check registers (or ask a local bank to donate them).

AND, the fourth week in January is also—

- ☆ **The beginning of National Scottish Culture Month**

JANUARY by the DAY

JANUARY 1 — Timing Peace Time

Each year at twelve noon GMT (Greenwich Mean Time), participants in this event give one hour to peace. People meditate, listen to peaceful music, read essays or poems about peace, discuss peace, or do any activity that encourages peace in the world. What a great idea! But if you wanted to participate, when would you do so? What time is it in your area when it is noon GMT? What time will it be in other parts of the U.S., where friends or family members might want to join in at the same time? Help children use a world map or globe with time zones on it to figure this out.

JANUARY 2 — Heights and Weights

It's the birthday of Lucia Zarate (1863–1889), the lightest known adult human. Born in Mexico, she weighed 2.5 pounds at birth. By the time she turned 20, she was $26\frac{1}{2}$ inches tall and weighed 20 pounds. Help children find classroom objects or benchmarks that match Lucia's weight or height.

JANUARY 3 — Straw Math

On this day in 1888, M. C. Stone of Washington, DC, got a patent for the first drinking straw. How long is a drinking straw anyway? Are all straws the same size? Take a "straw poll" to figure out how many families use straws regularly. Or try some straw estimates; such as, how many straws it would take to reach from your room to the principal's office or how many straws weigh one pound.

JANUARY 4 — Four-Wheelers

In 1863 James Plimpton of New York patented four-wheel roller skates, which changed personal transportation forever! Suppose Mr. Plimpton were to give a pair of four-wheel skates to each child in your class. How many wheels would he need?

JANUARY 6 — Common De-NAME-inator

It's National Smith Day! This event recognizes that Smith (and variations of it, such as Smythe or Goldsmith) is the most common last name in the English-speaking world. Sponsors estimate that there are over 2.3 million Smiths in the U.S. alone! Have children guess how many pages in your local telephone directory list Smiths. Then have groups of children take a Smith census: Find out how many Smiths are in your school. Is Smith the most common last name? If not, what is? How many in your school share the most common last name, whatever it is?

JANUARY 7   Long Distance Phone Math

It's the anniversary of the start of commercial transatlantic telephone service. This day in 1927 marked the first time people could make calls between New York and London. Thirty-one such calls were made that day. Have children find out the distance from New York to London and the approximate distance from your community to London. For a longer activity, you might use this day to begin a "telephone poll" to find out how many (if any) transatlantic telephone calls your students or their family members make or receive in a week or month.

JANUARY 8   Elvis Math

Happy Birthday, Elvis Presley (1935–1977), "king of rock n' roll." How old would Elvis be if he were still rockin' and rollin' today? He has been gone for over 20 years, but Elvis still holds music industry records (pun intended!): over 170 hit singles, over 80 top-selling albums, and 29 platinum records! He made his first recording in 1953. His first big hits came out in 1956. Invite students to use these statistics to make up math story problems about The King. For instance:

⊚ *How old was Elvis when he made his first recording?* (18)

⊚ *From his first hit, about how many hit singles did he have per year?* (about 8)

JANUARY 9   Tons of Math

On this day in 1956, the song "Sixteen Tons" by Tennessee Ernie Ford topped the pop music charts. So how much is 16 tons? Help children figure this out. (32,000 pounds) Then help them estimate about how many cars (school buses, elephants, whales, and so on) it would take to equal 16 tons. (BONUS: Today is the birthday of author Marcia Miller, who deeply loves this day.)

JANUARY 10 〉 Record Records

On this day in 1949, RCA introduced the first 45 rpm record. It was seven inches in diameter and had a large hole in the center. This new format changed the pop music industry. Help children draw circles that have 7-inch diameters. Have them compare these circles to the size of LP records (bring one in) or to CDs (which are about $4\frac{1}{2}$ inches in diameter and have a small hole in the center).

JANUARY 11 〉 Ten-Dollar Discoveries

Happy Birthday to Alexander Hamilton (1755 or 1757?–1804), the first Secretary of the Treasury of the United States. His portrait appears on the ten-dollar bill. Have children figure out how many different ways they could make $10 using only bills. (4: one $10; two $5; one $5 + five $1; ten $1) Then have them find out how many of each coin makes $10. (1000 pennies; 200 nickels; 100 dimes; 40 quarters; 20 half-dollars)

JANUARY 12 〉 Area Clean-Off

On or around this date, it's National Clean-Off-Your-Desk Day! If you participate in this event (held annually on the second Monday of January), you know that you'll have at least one day this year when your desktop is truly clean and clear! Today, have children find the area of their desktop or tabletop in square units. Use standard units, such as square inch or square centimeter, or nonstandard units, such as index cards (cut into 3 x 3 squares), color tiles, or any other manipulatives.

JANUARY 13 〉 Math in Poetry

Today is Poetry Break Day. Celebrate by reading a math poem to the class and inviting children to respond to it, act it out, or solve the problem it poses. Some suggestions include "Reflection," "Shapes," and "Smart" by Shel Silverstein; "The Song of the Shapes" by Charles Causley; or "Hands," "Measuring," "Autumn," and "Apples" by Avelyn Davidson.

JANUARY 15 〉 Teaching Math

Today is Elementary School Teacher Day. Celebrate by inviting children to take the role of teacher today. "Teachers" can tutor peer partners on math skills, teach math tricks or shortcuts they know, or demonstrate how to use computers, calculators, compasses, abacuses, or other math materials.

JANUARY 16 ⎰ Zero, Zilch, and Nada

Today is National Nothing Day! First observed in 1973, Harold Pullman Coffin created this event for "one national day when [Americans] can just sit without celebrating, observing, or honoring anything." For a simple twist on the idea, spend time today coming up with various ways to express zero. Examples include number sentences like 4 x 0 = 0, 27 − 27 = 0, or 1 + ¯1 = 0. Or have children list different expressions that mean "zero", such as *zilch, zip, null,* and so on.

JANUARY 18 ⎰ Pooh Poll

It's Pooh Day! Today is the birthday of A. A. Milne (1882–1956), author of the much-loved Winnie the Pooh stories. Take a survey to find out children's favorite Milne character: Is it Christopher Robin, Winnie, Piglet, Eeyore, Tigger, or another? You might extend the survey to include responses from children in other classes.

JANUARY 19 ⎰ Sea Lion Measures

It's time for San Francisco's annual Pier 39 Sea Lion "Haul Out." Each year since 1990, hundreds of California sea lions (*Zalophus Californianus*) have gathered at that pier on their migratory route. About 10,000 visitors come to see the sea lion habitat and learn about sea lion migration. Take time today to learn about these creatures. For instance, *how long is a typical California sea lion?* ($5\frac{1}{2}$ to $7\frac{1}{2}$ feet) *About how much does an adult male weigh?* (440–660 pounds) *An adult female?* (about 200 pounds) *About how many students would balance an adult male or female sea lion?*

JANUARY 20 ⎰ Compatible Coasters

On this day in 1885, L. A. Thompson of Coney Island, New York, got a patent for the roller coaster. Thompson's coaster was 450 feet long and its highest drop was 30 feet. Modern roller coasters can be a mile or more long; some have vertical drops of over 200 feet! Tell students that 1 mile = 5,280 feet. Use compatible numbers to help them estimate the length of Thompson's ride in fractions of a mile. (about 1/12 mile)

JANUARY 21 ⎰ Circumference Conference

Happy National Hugging Day! Remind children to hug their loved ones when they get home. At school, spend time using hugging as a way to investigate the circumference (distance around the outside) of large objects. For instance, how many children does it take to hug the biggest tree on your school grounds? How many does it take to hug a school bus? A piano? Have children hold hands to make a "child chain" that goes all the way around one or more of these objects.

JANUARY 22 | Meow Math

Today is Answer Your Cat's Question Day! Sponsors of this event believe that if you look closely at a cat, you can figure out what question it would like to ask you. Ask some cat-math questions today, such as: If I meow five times each hour, how many meows will I make in a day? (5 x 24 = 120). Or: If I eat 7 cans of Kitty Chow a week, and each can costs 49 cents, how much does it cost to feed me? ($3.43)

JANUARY 23 | Pies NOT to Eat

It's National Pie Day! But instead of celebrating by baking or eating pies, just focus on pie charts (circle graphs). Draw a circle to represent the six hours of a school day. Work with children to figure out what portion of the pie they spend reading, eating, writing, or working on certain subjects. Or work on a pie chart that represents a typical allowance a student in your class might receive. Work out what part of the money goes toward savings, snacks, gifts, and so on.

JANUARY 25 | Kernel Counts

On or around today (whenever it's Super Bowl Sunday), it's National Popcorn Day! Pose some popcorn related questions children can answer. For example:

⊙ *How many kernels are in 1 cup of unpopped corn?*

⊙ *How many popped corns are in 1 cup?*

⊙ *Which weighs more: 1 cup of corn unpopped or popped?*

⊙ *How many kernels of popcorn can you hold in one hand?*

JANUARY 27 | Mozart and Mental Math

Today is the birthday of Wolfgang Amadeus Mozart (1756–1791), who wrote more than 600 works in his lifetime. Mozart describes how he created pieces fully in his mind; notating them on paper was a chore to be finished after. Honor this great composer by doing some mental math today as his music plays in the background. A good choice is "Eine Kleine Nachtmusik" (A Little Night Music). Urge children to determine answers in their heads without using paper and pencil.

JANUARY 28 | Candle Power

In 1959 the song "Sixteen Candles" by The Crests, was #1 on the pop music charts. It was about a girl's sixteenth birthday. Pose the following problem to your class: Suppose we wanted to hold one huge birthday party for everyone in the class and we wanted enough candles for everybody's birthday cake. How many candles would we need?

JANUARY 29 | Puzzling Math

It's National Puzzle Day! Recognize the day by posing math puzzles. Here are a few:

- *Think of a number between 1 and 10. If you double it, it's even. But if you take half of it, it's odd. What is the number?* (2 or 6)

- *Seven coins make 25¢. There are no nickels. Name the coins.* (5 pennies, 2 dimes)

- *The day before yesterday was Sunday. What day is 3 days from today?* (Friday)

- *What number comes next? 1, 2, 3, 5, 8, 13, 21…* (34)

JANUARY 30 | Dime Time

Happy Birthday, Franklin D. Roosevelt (1882–1945), thirty-second President of the United States. Roosevelt's portrait appears on the dime. Today, do some activities with dimes. For instance, have students figure out how many dimes are in $1.80, $3.50, or $5.00. (18, 35, 50) Or have them estimate how many dimes placed edge to edge on a table form a line that is one foot long. (17) Children can also figure out the value of a stack of dimes that is as tall as one dime standing on its edge. ($1.40)

JANUARY 31 | Stuck on Math

On this day in 1928, Richard Drew of the 3M Company developed Scotch tape. Where would we be without that sticky stuff today? Have children make some math models today that are held together with Scotch tape. For example, they can form a cylinder by rolling a sheet of paper and taping the ends together. Or they can cut out the net below and fold and tape it together to form a cube.

Cube net: 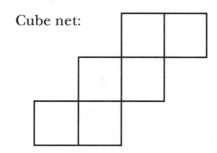 6 boxes you can fold to form a cube

February by the Month

Groundhogs, valentines, and presidents usually typify February. But there's much more to mark the shortest month of the year (even in leap years!). February is—

☺ **American Heart Month**
Everyone agrees that one way to stay heart-healthy is to exercise regularly. This month, have children keep track of the amount and kind of exercise they do each day. Compile the findings at the end of each week into a class chart or graph. Look for patterns, trends, or conclusions the data may suggest. Ask a doctor or nurse to talk to the class about ways to maintain a healthy heart.

☺ **International Embroidery Month**
Few people today embroider as a hobby, but in the past, most young girls did so. They often made samplers to practice their stitching. Have children make modern-day samplers using grid paper and Xs to represent the cross-stitch. Encourage them to weave math into their samplers. For example, they might make a sampler that displays tricky number facts, skip-counting patterns, definitions of math terms, or equivalences (such as 1 quart = 4 cups). Display the cross-stitch samplers around the room all month.

☺ **Return Shopping Carts to the Supermarket Month**
Did you know that the shopping cart was invented in Oklahoma in 1955? People often wheel groceries home in a shopping cart but somehow never get around to returning it. This event is to make people aware of the importance of taking back borrowed items such as shopping carts, milk crates, and bread trays. Borrow a shopping cart (but return it!), and display it in the classroom. Children can estimate how many books (shoes, backpacks, and so on) fit in the cart, how tall (wide, deep) it is, or how many times the wheels turn as the cart travels across the room. Help older children find its volume in cubic units.

AND, February is also—

☆ **Black History Month**

☆ **International Boost Self-Esteem Month**

☆ **National Cherry Month**

☆ **National Children's Dental Health Month**

☆ **National Wild Bird Feeding Month**

☆ **Plant the Seeds of Greatness Month**

☆ **Worldwide Innovation Month**

FEBRUARY by the WEEK

WEEK 1 — Global Family Feast Week

Celebrate the dazzling array of global foods all week long.

- ◎ **International Taste:** Bring in a representative food, ingredient, condiment, or spice from a different culture, country, or continent each day this week. As children taste the item, have them rank it from 1 to 10 according to how much they like it. Compile the data at week's end to see how the international foods fared.

- ◎ **Ethnic Menus:** Invite each child to bring in a family recipe that reflects his or her culture. Have children work in groups to multiply the ingredients listed in each recipe to serve everyone in the class. If possible, cook and prepare one or more of the recipes for a Global Class Feast.

AND, the first week in February is also—

- ☆ **National School Counseling Week**

WEEK 2 — National Kraut and Frankfurter Week

This event honors sauerkraut and franks as one of America's favorite taste combos.

- ◎ **Hot-Dog Math:** How many hot dogs would it take to serve everyone in the class? How many packs of franks would you have to buy? How much would it cost? If everyone in the class shared the cost, how much would each person contribute?

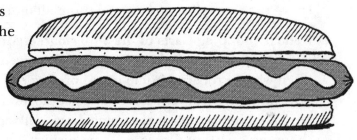

- ◎ **Match That Cabbage!** Sauerkraut is sliced cabbage fermented in water and salt. In 1989 a Welsh farmer grew the largest cabbage in the world. That huge head weighed in at 124 pounds! How many different ways can your students form groups whose combined weight is 124 pounds?

AND, the second week in February is also—

- ☆ **Celebration of Love Week**
- ☆ **Love Makes the World Go Round, but Laughter Keeps Us From Getting Dizzy Week**
- ☆ **National Child Passenger Safety Awareness Week**
- ☆ **Random Acts of Kindness Week**

56

WEEK 3 | Home for Birds Week

Winter can be rough on wild birds, so this week is a great time to focus on the needs of different kinds of birds in the wild.

⊚ **Migratory Maps:** Obtain maps that show the routes of various migratory birds. Help children use the map scale to estimate the distances the birds travel.

⊚ **Bird Feeders:** Make simple bird feeders this week. Recycle used milk cartons as bird feeders by cutting an opening for the birds to enter, adding birdseed to the carton, and hanging it by string or wire from a tree branch. Or use a pinecone, peanut butter, and birdseed to create an organic bird feeder. Press peanut butter into the openings of the pine cone, roll the sticky cone into birdseed, and hang it outside. Describe this activity mathematically by measuring or weighing the ingredients or materials, charting the number of birds that visit your feeders, determining the price per feeder, calculating total cost, and so on.

AND, the third week in February is also—

☆ **Give Yourself Credit Week**

☆ **International Flirting Week**

☆ **International Friendship Week**

WEEK 4 | National Engineers Week

This event acknowledges and encourages technical thinking. Present these simple engineering challenges to students any time this week.

⊚ **Bridge Math:** Form a 6-inch open space between two desks or chairs. Using just paper, how can you create a bridge over that space that can support a paperback book? (One way is to roll paper tightly into a tube, lay two such tubes across the space, and balance the book on them.)

⊚ **Ramp Test:** How far will a ball roll off a 10-inch ramp? What factors influence how far the ball rolls? How can you increase the distance?

AND, the fourth week in February is also—

☆ **National FFA (Future Farmers of America) Week**

FEBRUARY by the DAY

FEBRUARY 1 \ Jump and Count

On this day in 1990, India's Vadivelu Karunakaren set a world's record for skip-run jumping rope. He covered 10 miles in 58 minutes! Have a contest in the gym or on the school yard. How many times can children jump rope (in a stationary position) without missing? How many times if they are moving forward? Have partners count for each other. Record the data on a class chart or line plot.

FEBRUARY 2 \ Kiwi Math

It's California Kiwifruit Day! Celebrate by serving kiwis to your class. Before you cut the delicious fruits, have children weigh them and measure their lateral and longitudinal distances with a tape measure. Kiwis have about 75 calories per fruit. If you wanted to have a 300-calorie lunch, how many kiwis could you eat? (4)

FEBRUARY 3 \ Math Merriment

On or around today (annually the first Tuesday in February) is Laugh and Grow Rich Day! Sponsors of this event believe that laughter improves a person's chances for success. Pose this silly math riddle to your class today: *How much dirt is there in a hole 1 foot deep, 1 foot wide, and 1 foot long?* (None—a hole has no dirt in it!)

FEBRUARY 4 \ Midpoints

Today is winter's midpoint. Winter is half over—or you could say that it's halfway to spring. Spend time thinking about other midpoints today. For instance:

When is the midpoint of the school day? Of the school year? Of this month? When is the midpoint of your lunch break? Of math class?

FEBRUARY 5 \ Homer Projection

Happy Birthday, Hank Aaron (b. 1934). He holds the record for the most home runs hit in a career by a Major League Baseball player. The record, set in 1976, is 755 homers. Pose this question to students: *Suppose you hit 1 home run each week from now on. How many years would it take you to tie Aaron's record?* (about $14\frac{1}{2}$ years)

FEBRUARY 6 | Math Appreciation

Today is Pay-a-Compliment Day. "Go ahead, make someone feel a little happier today," say the sponsors of this event. Take time today to acknowledge any kind of mathematical thinking that goes on outside regular math time. For instance, you use math to take milk count, to figure out how much time is left until lunch, to determine how many scissors to borrow from the art teacher, and so on. Encourage students to point out whenever math comes into use. Pay compliments to the math and to those who recognize its importance all around us.

FEBRUARY 7 | Math from the Prairie

Happy Birthday to Laura Ingalls Wilder (1867–1957), author of the eight *Little House* books. Honor pioneer life by making some simple pioneer foods mentioned in the books. An excellent source for recipes is *The Little House Cookbook: Frontier Foods from Laura Ingalls Wilder's Classic Stories.* Suggestions include homemade lemonade, johnny cakes, or biscuits. Or read aloud a passage from one of Wilder's books in which she describes an old-fashioned school.

FEBRUARY 9 | Count the Days

Happy Birthday, William Henry Harrison (1793–1841), our ninth president. He held office the shortest time of any U.S. president—just 32 days. He caught pneumonia during his inauguration ceremonies and died of complications soon after. Harrison took office on March 4, 1841. When did his presidency end? (April 4)

FEBRUARY 10 | Countdown to Safety

On this day in 1863, Alanson Crane of Virginia got a patent for the first fire extinguisher in America. Today, examine the fire extinguisher nearest to your classroom. Check the date it was last inspected to figure out when its next inspection is due. Help children figure out how long it has been since it was inspected and how long it will be before the next inspection.

FEBRUARY 12 | Penny Hunt

It's Lost Penny Day. This event coincides with the birthday of Abraham Lincoln (1809–1865), whose portrait appears on the U.S. penny. Event sponsors ask people to gather lost pennies from under cushions, on the bottom of purses, in pockets, behind furniture, wherever. Once people collect them, they are advised to donate them to a worthy cause. You might hold a lost penny search in your classroom to see how many pennies children can find, and vote on where to donate the money. Or invite children to conduct a lost penny search at home and take a class tally, even if the pennies are not brought to school.

FEBRUARY 13 | Old School

On this day in 1635, the Boston Latin School opened it doors for the first time. It is America's oldest public school. Just how old is it? How does its age compare with the age of your school?

FEBRUARY 14 | Seating Capacity

Along with being Valentine's Day, today is also Ferris Wheel Day. This event honors the birth of George Washington Gale Ferris (1859–1896), the engineer who invented the ride that bears his name. The Ferris wheel first appeared in 1893 in Chicago. Its huge wheel was 250 feet in diameter. It had 36 coaches, each of which could hold 40 riders. It was a huge hit! Today's largest Ferris wheel is bigger (328 feet in diameter), but each of its 60 gondolas seats just 8 people. Compare the capacity of the two Ferris wheels. (1,440, 480) Could everyone in your school ride either of these two Ferris wheels at once?

FEBRUARY 15 | Mustard Math

Here it is again—Mustard Day! On this day in 1758, Benjamin Franklin advertised mustard for the first time in America. Take a mustard survey. On what foods is mustard the condiment of choice? Ask your classroom gourmets whether they prefer yellow mustard, brown mustard, spicy mustard, or no mustard at all. Graph the results.

FEBRUARY 17 | Quadrilaterals

Happy Birthday to actor Lou Diamond Phillips (b. 1962). Figure out how old he is today. To celebrate his birthday, investigate the properties of all the four-sided shapes that children know, including the diamond, square, rectangle, trapezoid, rhombus, parallelogram, and irregular quadrilateral. Have them classify the ones that have right angles (square corners), the ones that have equal sides, the ones that look the same whether you flip, turn, or slide them, and so on.

FEBRUARY 18 | Milk Math

Well, it's time again for the Elm Farm Ollie Day Celebration! On this day in 1930, Ollie became the first cow to fly in an airplane. During her flight, a farmer milked her, sealed the milk in paper cartons, and parachuted them over St. Louis! To honor this brave bovine, find out more about milk products. For instance:

     ⚅ *How many calories are in 1 cup of whole milk, 2% milk, 1% milk, and skim milk?*

     ⚅ *How many cups are in a quart of milk? In a half-gallon? In a gallon?*

     ⚅ *How many cups of milk does it take to make 1 cup of cheese?*

FEBRUARY 19 | Lend Me Your Numerals!

Today is the fiftieth day of the year. What better time to introduce or review L, the Roman numeral for 50! Model how to write Roman numerals from 40 (XL), the first number to use L, through 89 (LXXXIX), the last number below 100 to use it.

FEBRUARY 20 | Math Volunteers

Today is Student Volunteer Day. This event honors students who donate their time to help others. Anyone can be a student volunteer. Today, why not arrange for your students to volunteer as math tutors to younger children in your school? Older kids can help younger ones count, sort, or order objects. They can check their work, or you might drill them on math facts. Chart the types of volunteer activities students engage in.

FEBRUARY 21 | Monumental Math

On this day in 1885, the Washington Monument was dedicated. The famous obelisk is 555 feet $5\frac{1}{2}$ inches tall, rising from a base that is 55 feet $1\frac{1}{2}$ inches square. An obelisk is a four-sided pillar that tapers as it rises and ends in a pyramid. Display a photograph of the monument. To help children get a feel for how big it is, mark out a 55 foot $1\frac{1}{2}$-inch square on a field near school. Gather students inside the square. Tell them that there are 898 steps inside that visitors can climb to reach eight small observation windows near the top. If everyone in your school stood on a different step inside the monument, how many steps would remain empty? Or find out the height of the tallest building, monument, or tower in your area. Compare its height to that of the Washington Monument.

FEBRUARY 22 | Record Height

Happy Birthday to Robert Pershing Wadlow (1918–1940), the world's tallest man. He was over 6 feet tall by the time he was ten years old. At his death, he measured 8 feet 11.1 inches in height. Measure up a wall to mark Wadlow's amazing height. Wadlow's arm span was 9 feet $5\frac{1}{2}$ inches across, his feet were $18\frac{1}{2}$ inches long, and his hands measured $12\frac{1}{2}$ inches from wrist to fingertip. Have each child make a chart comparing his or her height, arm span, foot length, and hand length to his.

FEBRUARY 24 ⏐ Math Tales

It's Once Upon a Time Day! It occurs today on the birthday of Wilhelm Grimm (1786–1859), who, with his brother Jacob (1785–1863), published volumes of German fairy tales that captivated children around the world. Celebrate by inviting children to create a math fairy tale in which they present a story problem in fairy tale style. Or read aloud a math fairy tale, such as *Melisande* by E. Nesbit, *The King's Chessboard* by David Birch, or *A Grain of Rice* by Helena Pittman.

FEBRUARY 26 ⏐ Canyon Depth

On this day in 1919, an act of Congress established the Grand Canyon National Park in Arizona. Display pictures of this spectacular national treasure, along with these facts: The elevation at the Colorado River is 2,400 feet above sea level. The elevation at the South Rim Village, where the Visitors Center is located and where many trails begin, is 7,498 feet above sea level. *What is the difference in elevation from the canyon, top to bottom? Is this more or less than a mile?* (182 feet less; 5280–5098) *Would you rather climb down into the canyon or up from the river to the rim? Why?*

FEBRUARY 28 ⏐ Flower Power

It's Floral Design Day, an event that honors the art of flower arranging and design. Add some flowers to your math lessons today. For example: Present story problems about flowers, petals, leaves, or blossoms. Tell children that the fastest growing flowering plant, the *hesperoyucca whipplei*, can grow at a rate of 10 inches a day! At that rate, when would your students reach a height of 6 feet? The world's largest flower is the *Rafflesia arnoldi* of southeast Asia. Its blossom can grow up to 3 feet across and weighs as much as 36 pounds! What common objects match its size and weight?

FEBRUARY 29 ⏐ Leap Year Day

If there's a leap day this year, talk about what people do who were actually born on this day. Most celebrate their birthdays on February 28 or March 1 during nonleap-years. But some, like Frederick, the main character in The Pirates of Penzance, believe that they must be only one fourth as old as the rest of us! Leap Day births include American astronaut Jack Lousma (b. 1936), Russian Olympic cross-country skier Raisa Smetanina (b. 1952), and actor Antonio Sabato, Jr. (b. 1972).

MARCH by the MONTH

Shamrocks aren't the only special shapes associated with March. Don't forget kidney and umbrella shapes! You might be surprised to learn that March is—

☺ **Music in Our Schools Month**

What better way to memorize things than to learn the lyrics of songs! Music is an excellent motivator for most children— adults too! Spend time this month singing math songs. If your students are learning their multiplication facts, get a copy of *Times Tunes* by Marcia Miller (Scholastic). Or obtain tapes of rap tunes that present number facts. Better yet, work with students to take well-known melodies and create original lyrics for them that feature math concepts suitable to the topics you're studying. Look for musical patterns involving rhythm, melody, or harmony.

☺ **National Craft Month**

This event promotes the fun and creativity of handcrafts of all kinds. It's a great month for math crafts. Use your creativity and help from your school art teacher to come up with math crafts for this month. Some familiar projects include making geoboards out of scrap wood and nails. Children can explore symmetry and patterns by doing beadwork or weaving. They'll experience congruence firsthand by making rubbings of textured objects. They can learn about parabolic curves by doing string art projects. Happy crafting!

☺ **National Sauce Month**

This event celebrates the diversity of sauces used in all kinds of cooking. Make some sauces with your class. Many require no cooking, such as Thai peanut sauce, Italian pesto, or Mexican pico de gallo. Others, like Italian spaghetti sauce or Chinese duck sauce require cooking, but no fancy kitchen skills. Make some sauces with your class, or have a Sauce-Off and ask children to bring in their favorite sauces so that classmates can taste them on crackers, veggies, rice, or pasta.

AND, March is also—

☆ **Irish-American Heritage Month**   ☆ **National Women's History Month**

☆ **National Kidney Month**   ☆ **Youth Art Month**

☆ **National Umbrella Month**

March by the Week

Week 1 | National School Breakfast Week

Breakfast, whether eaten at home or in school, is an important way to "start our engines" each morning. Think about breakfast at the start of this month.

- ⊚ **Breakfast Combos:** Have children make up menu combinations for breakfasts by selecting one item from each of these categories: (1) pancakes or cereal, (2) fruit or juice, (3) toast or muffin, and (4) milk or cocoa. Well, someone could have cereal with fruit, toast, and cocoa, while another has pancakes, juice, muffin, and milk. Have the class come up with as many different breakfast combos as they can.

- ⊚ **Toast Test:** Suppose you have a class breakfast at school and everyone will have two pieces of toast. How many loaves of bread should you get to be sure that there is enough for everyone? How does the answer change if you want to serve different kinds of bread, or if you buy different brands of bread?

AND, the first week in March is also—

- ☆ **Help Someone See Week**
- ☆ **National Procrastination Week**
- ☆ **National Professional Pet Sitters Week**
- ☆ **Return Your Borrowed Books Week**

Week 2 | Autograph Collecting Week

Where's the math in autograph collecting? It may be in the prices people earn or fees they pay, how many autographs they have, or how long (or short) the names are. Try some of these activities this week.

- ⊚ **Consonant and Vowel Counts:** Have children sign their autograph and then analyze it for number of consonants and vowels. Help them express each amount as a fraction. For instance, A. Lincoln, (as our sixteenth president usually signed his name) has 8 letters, of which 3 are vowels ($\frac{3}{8}$) and 5 are consonants ($\frac{5}{8}$).

- ⊚ **Autograph Wish List:** From which famous people would children most like to have an autograph? Take a survey and display the results in a chart or graph.

AND, the second week in March is also—

- ☆ **Girl Scout Week**
- ☆ **Universal Women's Week**

WEEK 3 | Go Nuts Over Peanuts Week

Texas is our second largest peanut producer, and it's one of only two states to grow all four American varieties: Runner, Spanish, Valencia, and Virginia.

⑥ **Goober Graph:** Which do you prefer: salted or unsalted peanuts? Peanuts in the shell or out? Plain or flavored peanuts? Gather class data and graph the results. Celebrate with a peanut butter party!

⑥ **Peanut Proportions:** Half of all American peanuts are made into peanut butter, and a fourth are roasted. Give each group a bag or handful of peanuts in the shell. Have them divide the peanuts to accurately reflect this data.

AND, the third week in March is also—

☆ **Children's Healthcare Week**

☆ **National Agriculture Week**

☆ **National Manufacturing Week**

☆ **National Poison Prevention Week**

WEEK 4 | National Sports Trivia Week

Any fan can tell you that math abounds in athletics data. This week is a great time to add sports stats to your math classes.

⑥ **Sports Trivia Problems:** Encourage children to make up questions about sport stats. They can involve comparing numbers, batting averages, length of careers, speeds, scores, whatever! Groups can present problems to one another and solve them together, or you can post the questions as problems of the day.

⑥ **Guinness Greats:** One source of sports data is the annual Guinness Book of Records. Obtain several copies of this book and have groups look through it to find interesting sports math. For instance, the men's world record for barrel jumping on ice skates is 29 feet 5 inches over 18 barrels, and the women's record for the same event is 22 feet $5\frac{1}{2}$ inches over 11 barrels. Compare these records.

AND, the fourth week in March is also—

☆ **National Clutter Awareness Week**

☆ **National Week of the Ocean Festival Sea-Son**

MARCH by the DAY

MARCH 1 — Porcine Play

It's National Pig Day! Sponsors of this event want to promote the idea that the pig is an intelligent and useful animal (despite its bad reputation!). This is a good day to play the math game "Buzz!"—renamed as "Oink!" Players sit in a circle and begin to count off. Whenever the number to be said is a multiple of 7 (substitute another rule, if you wish), the child replaces that number with a resounding "Oink!" and the next child picks up the count.

MARCH 2 — Quintessential Math

On this day in 1987, two sets of healthy quintuplets were born in the U.S.: the Helms babies in Peoria, Illinois, and the Jenkins kids in Las Vegas, Nevada. Take five today to brainstorm other words that use the prefix *quint-*, which means "five." Examples include *quintet, quints, quintillion,* and *quintuplicate.* Help students determine their meanings.

MARCH 3 — Star-Spangled Math

Today is National Anthem Day. On this day in 1931, the U.S. Senate passed a bill declaring "The Star-Spangled Banner" as our national anthem. President Herbert Hoover signed the bill that same day. Try some star math today. For example: How many points are on all the stars on our flag today? (5 x 50 = 250) Or have children estimate how long it takes to sing "The Star-Spangled Banner" all the way through. Record their estimates. Then sing the anthem together as you time it.

MARCH 4 — Function Machines

March 4 is the only date that gives a command ("March Forth!" Get the pun?) Today is a good day to present function machines, which operate on any number by commanding it to follow its rule. For example, if the rule on a function machine is "Add 4," then any number that goes in comes out 4 greater. You can draw a simple function machine on the board, or make one out of an old box. First, present the rule and have children determine the output; then, present the output and have children determine the rule.

MARCH 6 \ Tall and Taller

Happy Birthday to basketball star Shaquille O'Neal (b. 1972). At 7 feet 1 inch, "Shaq" (pronounced *shack*) towers over his opponents. Help children restate his height in inches. (85 in.) Challenge more advanced students to restate Shaq's height in nonconventional ways, such as 4 feet 37 inches.

MARCH 7 \ Monopoly Money

Legend has it that on this day in 1933, Charles B. Darrow of Pennsylvania invented the game *Monopoly*. He sold his first games soon thereafter, and the game hasn't stopped selling since! Have children figure out the total number of bills and amount of money each player gets at the start of the game, based on *Monopoly* rules: 2 each of $500, $100, and $50 bills, 6 $20 bills, and 5 each of $10, $5, and $1 bills. (27 bills that total $1,500). Extend by figuring out how many bills of each denomination the class would need if everyone played and how much money that would be.

MARCH 9 \ Time in Space

Today is the birthday of Yuri Gagarin (1934–1968), the first human ever to travel into space (April 12, 1961). Gagarin's historic flight lasted 108 minutes. Set a time for a countdown, as if your class were rocketing into space. Once you achieve liftoff, figure out the exact time of your landing.

MARCH 10 \ Date That Name!

It's MARIO Day! Why? Because you can abbreviate the date as MAR 10, which looks a lot like the name Mario! This event was invented by a guy named—you guessed it! Challenge children to think of another date when this circumstance could occur. (Examples include March 15 for Maris and July 10 for Julio.)

MARCH 11 \ Hand Signals

The Bureau of Indian Affairs (BIA) was created on this day in 1824. It was the part of the U.S. War Department whose job was to work out peaceful settlements between Native and other Americans. Later the BIA became a separate agency. Today, teach children the sign language shared by many different tribes of American Indians who lived on the Great Plains. Discuss ways in which their signals are similar to or different from analogous hand signals your students use.

MARCH 12 \ Blizzards and Snowdrifts

Early this morning in 1888, snow began falling in the northeastern United States and didn't stop until there were nearly 50 inches covering the ground! The extreme winds of "The Great Blizzard of 88" left snowdrifts as high as 40 feet! With your class, determine which classroom or personal objects would be completely covered by 50 inches of snow and which would be partially covered. Which students would be tall enough to peer out over the top of such a snowfall?

MARCH 14 \ Circular Reasoning

It's Pi Day! *Pi* (π), the mathematical constant 3.141592..., is the ratio of the circumference of a circle to its diameter. The value of *pi*, rounded to the nearest hundredth, matches a shortcut way to write today's date (3/14). No need to run in circles today. Just try some hands-on investigations of the properties of circles. For instance, here's a circle check. Place a coin, counter, Pog, or any other round object on a table. How many objects of the same size can you place around the first one so that all sides touch? Does the size of the object matter? (6, regardless of diameter)

MARCH 15 \ Blowout Scores

On this day in 1869, the Cincinnati Red Stockings, America's first professional baseball team, routed its opponents by a score of 41–7. How many more runs would the losing team have to have scored to win that lopsided game? (35)

MARCH 16 \ Feathery Fourths

It's Curlew Day at Umatilla National Wildlife Refuge in Oregon. Hundreds of these graceful wading birds find their way here to nest each year. The long-billed curlew has a slender, down-curving bill that is about one quarter its total length. For example, you'd see a 6-inch bill on a 24-inch-long curlew. Present curlew Qs (Get it?!) like these:

     ⊚ *If a curlew is 48 centimeters long, how long is its bill?* (12 centimeters)

     ⊚ *A curlew with a 4-inch bill is how long in all?* (16 inches)

MARCH 17 \ Pear Geometry

On this day in 1958, Vanguard I, the world's first solar-powered satellite, proved that the earth is not a perfectly shaped ball (sphere) but is actually an *oblate spheroid* or pear-shaped *ellipsoid*. Display models of spheres and pears so children can discern and describe the differences. Then have children mold a small earth with modeling clay. They can start with as perfect a ball as they can form. Then tell them that the equator (the imaginary belt around the middle of the earth) bulges out a little, as does the North Pole, but that the South Pole is slightly indented.

MARCH 19 \ Time Zones

On this day in 1918, Congress authorized establishing time zones for the United States. The act also set up "Daylight Saving Time," when we turn clocks ahead one hour in the spring and back one hour in the fall. Display a U.S. map that shows time zones. Find out which time zone your community is in. Then have children name other cities or destinations around the United States and figure out the time zone for each place named. Help younger children simply determine whether it is earlier or later in other times zones. Older children can help them find the time in each place.

MARCH 20 \ Spring Sun Time

On or around this day, spring begins. (So does National Spring Fever Week!) Its arrival coincides with the vernal (spring) equinox, the time when the amount of time between sunrise and sunset is virtually the same everywhere on earth (except for the poles). Check the newspaper so you can post the exact times of sunrise and sunset today. Help children figure out how many hours of sunlight there are today.

MARCH 21 \ New Math Terms

Don't forget—it's Memory Day today! Acknowledge this occasion by having children memorize some lesser-known math facts. For example, help them learn that a *ream* of paper has 500 sheets, a *fortnight* is 2 weeks, and a *score* is a group of 20 things.

MARCH 22 \ Goofing Off

It's International Goof-Off Day! Sponsors encourage participants to have some fun and be a little silly. This is a good day to play math games. Just don't tell the children that they are learning as they play!

MARCH 23   Hasty Math

Today in 1950, a new TV game show had its premiere. *Beat the Clock* challenged contestants to complete stunts before the time ran out. This might be a good day to give a timed quiz of number facts or to time children as they race against the clock to complete a math puzzle or maze. Announce a reasonable time limit, such as one minute, and tell them that they must stop when the time runs out. You might want to repeat the same timed activity another time to see how children progress.

MARCH 25   Nuts and Bowls

It's Pecan Day! This event honors the day in 1775 when George Washington planted pecan trees at his home in Mount Vernon. Some of these trees still stand today. (And you associated Washington only with cherry trees!) It's a good day to bake a batch of pecan cookies or pecan bread. Or have children estimate the number of pecans in a bag, jar, or bowl.

MARCH 26   Creative Celebrating

Today is Make Up Your Own Holiday Day. Weave together language arts, social studies, and math by presenting this challenge to your class. Children can devise a holiday; make up a reason for it; create a slogan, poem, song, mascot, or greeting card for it; and determine what day it will fall on over the next several years.

MARCH 27   Counting Lyrics

Dr. Patty Smith Hill (1868–1946), whose birthday is today, helped start a world-wide musical tradition. She and her sister Mildred cowrote "Happy Birthday to You." Mildred composed the tune and Patty penned the lyrics. People say it is the most frequently sung song in the world, with lyrics in scores of languages. Have children figure out how many times they'd sing the word *birthday* if they sang this song to each person in the class. (Decide what to do if two birthdays fall on the same day.)

MARCH 29   Pitcher Perfect

Each year Major League Baseball honors its best National League and American League pitchers with the Cy Young Award—named for today's birthday boy. Cy Young (1867–1955) is the "winningest" pitcher in baseball history. He also pitched the first "perfect game." In a perfect game, no batter ever reaches first base. This is a rare accomplishment. Challenge students to figure out how many batters Cy Young faced during his perfect game. (27: 3 per inning, 9 innings) Would this number be the same in a little league game?

MARCH 30 ⎸ Pencil Poll

On this day in 1858, Hyman Lipman got a patent for a pencil with an eraser on top. His design, in which a metal band held a rubber eraser to the top of the pencil, is still used in pencils nowadays. Today, take a class pencil poll: *Who prefers to use a long pencil? A short pencil? A sharp pencil? A dull pencil? An ordinary pencil? A mechanical pencil?* Present findings in a graph or chart. Challenge children to ask and answer questions based on the data.

MARCH 31 ⎸ Tower to Scale

One of the world's most recognizable landmarks, the Eiffel Tower in Paris, was dedicated on this day in 1889. Without its modern radio antenna, the tower is 300 meters tall. Help children make a scale drawing of the tower on centimeter grid paper. Have each box stand for 20 meters, and count by twenties with children to determine the number of boxes they need to represent the tower. (15).

APRIL by the MONTH

Showers, fools, buds, breezes—April suggests new beginnings, fragrant blossoms, and dreams that summer isn't far off. But April is also—

⑥ **Listening Awareness Month**

Work to improve children's listening skills this month by reading aloud math stories that fit your program. Or present problems orally with the 1-2-3 method:

> *1. Read the problem once through so children can get the main idea.*
>
> *2. Now read the problem again, slowly, so children can extract the key details.*
>
> *3. Then read it a third time so children can verify their thinking.*

⑥ **National Poetry Month**

Celebrate this event by reading, creating, reciting, and recording math poems. Ask your school librarian for help, or contact the Academy of American Poets on the Internet at http://www.poets.org.

⑥ **ZAM! Zoo and Aquarium Month**

This event highlights the key role zoos and aquariums play in promoting wildlife education and conservation. It's the perfect time for zoo or ocean math, which might take the form of story problems about zoo or ocean animals, data analysis projects that involve comparisons of animal or ocean statistics, or research projects in which children gather statistics about animals or oceans.

AND, April is also—

☆ **Alcohol Awareness Month**

☆ **Classical Music Month**

☆ **Fresh Florida Tomato Month**

☆ **International Amateur Radio Month**

☆ **National Humor Month**

☆ **National Youth Sports Safety Month**

APRIL by the WEEK

WEEK 1 — Golden Rule Week

It's always wise to review the Golden Rule: Do to others as you'd have them do to you. But you can also examine mathematical rules anytime this week. For example:

☉ **Golden Ratio:** The Golden Ratio (or *divine proportion*) describes a particular relationship between the length and width of a rectangle that the Greeks believed to be most aesthetically pleasing. Common examples of items whose sizes follow the Golden Ratio are 3 x 5 and 5 x 8 index cards and the facade of the Parthenon. Display rectangles of various proportions and ask children which ones most please their eyes.

☉ **Equivalent Fractions:** Students who study fractions learn to simplify or reduce a fraction to its lowest terms (or to create an equivalent fraction in higher terms). One way to do so is to divide (or multiply) the numerator and the denominator by the same number. To help them remember this process, nickname it the Golden Rule of Fractions: "Be fair to numerators and to denominators." Demonstrate how to apply this rule as students practice this aspect of fraction calculation.

AND, the first week in April is also—

☆ **Global Communications Era Week**
☆ **National Birthplace Week**

WEEK 2 — National Reading a Road Map Week

☉ **Trip Planning:** Provide road maps of your state. Invite groups to plan a trip from your community to anywhere they choose. Have them determine a route and estimate the total driving distance using the map scale.

☉ **Math Maps:** Invite artistic learners to create original maps of imaginary places, including distances between towns, sites, or landmarks. For example, they might make a map of a rain forest region with spots like Panther Creek, Slothberg, and Parrotville. Exchange or display maps so children can make up and solve story problems based on the information they present.

AND, the second week in April is also—

☆ **International Building Safety Week**

☆ **National Garden Week**

☆ **National Public Health Week**

WEEK 3 〉 National Week of the Ocean

Use oceans, seas, and marine life for math projects anytime this week.

⊙ **Ocean Multiplication:** Read *Sea Squares* by Joy N. Hulme this week. This delightful picture book uses marine creatures to illustrate the concept of square numbers. (1 x 1 = 1, 2 x 2 = 4, 3 x 3 = 9, 4 x 4 = 16,…10 x 10 = 100)

⊙ **How Deep Is the Ocean?** Well, that depends on where you measure. Work with students to find the greatest depths or average depths of the world's oceans and seas. Consult an almanac. Present the data in the form of a graph or chart.

AND, the third week in April is also—

☆ **Pan American Week**

☆ **National Organize Your Files Week**

☆ **Talking Book Week**

WEEK 4 〉 National Coin Week

There's almost no limit to the coin problems children can puzzle over this week.

⊙ **Coin Questions:** Create coin problems children can solve by guessing and testing or by using play money. For instance: *What 3 coins make 45¢?* (1 quarter, 2 dimes) *With 4 different coins, what amounts of money might you have?*

⊙ **Chunks of Change:** As of 1997, over $24 billion in coins circulated in the United States. Of this, about $2 billion were silver dollars and the rest were pennies, nickels, dimes, quarters, and half-dollars. Can you imagine?! Invite students to make up little problems based on this big information.

AND, the fourth week in April is also—

☆ **National Library Week**

☆ **National Playground Safety Week**

☆ **National Volunteer Week**

☆ **National Welding Week**

☆ **Reading Is Fun Week**

☆ **Sky Awareness Week**

☆ **Week of the Young Child**

APRIL by the DAY

APRIL 2 — Penny Line

Today is the anniversary of the establishment of the first U.S. Mint (1792) in Philadelphia, Pennsylvania. The mint is where coins are made. Challenge children to estimate how many pennies placed end-to-end in a row are as long as they are tall. What would its value be?

APRIL 3 — Express Rates

On this day in 1860, the first Pony Express rider left St. Joseph, Missouri for Sacramento, California. This express delivery service promised to deliver letters within ten days at a cost of $5 per ounce. The Pony Express was in business until October 1861, when telegraph service became widely available. Weigh a math book. Figure out how much the Pony Express would have charged you to send it to a friend in California.

APRIL 4 — RDA of C

In 1932 University of Pittsburgh scientist C. C. King first isolated vitamin C on this day. The RDA (recommended daily allowance) of vitamin C for kids 7–10 years of age is 45 milligrams. Suppose seedless green grapes were your only source of vitamin C. Five grapes provide 1 mg of vitamin C. How many grapes would you have to eat to get your RDA of C? (225 grapes) Work with children to find more reasonable sources of vitamin C.

APRIL 6 — Olympics Count

On this day in 1896 in Athens, Greece, the first modern Olympic Games opened after a 1500-year gap. This summer international athletics event is held every four years. Help children figure out how many (summer) Olympic Games have been held to date. Note: No games were held in 1916, 1940, and 1944 due to international wars.

APRIL 7 — Mess Makers

Today is No Housework Day! Sponsors of this event invite us to take a day off from laundry, cleaning, doing dishes, and making beds. Pose this challenge to children: *If you made*

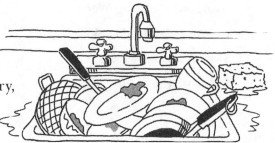

76

your bed every day since your last birthday, how many times would you have made the bed? Work together to figure out a solution plan.

APRIL 9 ⎫ Civil War Years

On this day in 1865, Confederate General Robert E. Lee surrendered to Union General Ulysses S. Grant, ending the War Between the States. That war, which began on April 12, 1861, was the bloodiest war ever fought on American soil. Help children figure out how long the war officially lasted. (3 days short of 4 years, or 1,458 days; 1864 was a leap year.)

APRIL 10 ⎫ Century Challenges

As long as this isn't a leap year, today is Day 100—the one hundredth day of the year. (If this IS a leap year, Day 100 fell on April 9). Try some activities today that are based on 100. For example:

- ⊚ *How long does it take to count aloud to 100?*
- ⊚ *How long does it take to write all the numbers from 1 to 100?*
- ⊚ *How long is a chain of 100 paper clips?*
- ⊚ *What was the date of the one hundredth day of your life?*

APRIL 11 ⎫ Quartet Questions

Today is Barbershop Quartet Day! On this day in 1938, 26 people gathered in Tulsa, Oklahoma, to form SPEBQSA: the Society for the Preservation and Encouragement of Barbershop Quartet Singing in America. How many barbershop quartets could you form in your class? What other things usually come in quartets?

APRIL 12 ⎫ Attendance Fines

In 1853 New York enacted the nation's first truancy law. According to this law, parents had to pay a $50 fine if their children (ages 5 to 15) were absent from school. (There were exceptions for illness or other emergencies.) Suppose that law were in effect today. How much money would the families in your class owe for all absences recorded today? (Count every absence, regardless of the reason.) For the week thus far? For all of last week?

APRIL 13 ⎫ Nickels Add Up

Happy Birthday to Thomas Jefferson (1743–1826), third president of the United States. Jefferson's portrait appears on the nickel. If you were to get a nickel for each year that has passed since Jefferson's birth, how much money would you have?

APRIL 14 ⟩ Lexicography Increase

Today in 1828, Noah Webster published his masterwork, *The American Dictionary of the English Language.* His great legacy, published in two volumes, presented about 70,000 entries. Today's modern English dictionaries contain nearly a half-million. Help children figure the increase in entries of the new dictionaries over Webster's original work.

APRIL 15 ⟩ Sales Tax

Today is Income Tax Pay Day. Although most children are unaware of the meaning of income tax, most are acquainted with sales tax. Work together to make a simple chart that shows the sales tax in your area. (If there is none, make a table for a common amount such as 4% or 5%. Explain that this means that for every dollar spent, you pay an extra 4 or 5 cents.) Present some exercises in which children use the chart to calculate the sales tax on dream purchases.

APRIL 16 ⟩ Whistling Times

On or around this date is the annual International Whistler's Convention. Celebrate by having a whistling contest. For instance, time how long children can sustain a whistled tone before they run out of breath. How many times through can they whistle a familiar tune like "Happy Birthday" or "Row, Row, Row Your Boat"?

APRIL 18 ⟩ Fan Figures

On this day in 1923, about 74,000 baseball fans went to the opening game at brand-new Yankee Stadium in the Bronx. Today the stadium's official seating capacity is 57,545. How many more fans were there on the original opening day? (about 16,455)

APRIL 19 ⟩ Marathon Minutes

On this day in 1897, John J. McDermott beat out his 14 competitors to win the first Boston Marathon. This race is the world's oldest annual marathon. McDermott's winning time was 2 hours, 55 minutes, 10 seconds (2:55:10). The course record, set in 1994 by Cosmas Ndeti of Kenya, is 2:07:15. Help children figure out how much faster Ndeti's time is than McDermott's. (47:55)

APRIL 20 } Creative Columns

Today is the birthday of sculptor Daniel Chester French (1850–1931). He is best known for his statue of a seated Abraham Lincoln, which is displayed in the Lincoln Memorial in Washington, DC. When the memorial was built, its marble outer building was designed to have 32 columns, one for each of the states in the Union at the time of Lincoln's death. If the memorial were being redesigned today, how many more columns would be needed to show the current number of states? (18)

APRIL 21 } Roman Candles

In Italy today is a national holiday celebrating the founding of Rome. By tradition, Rome was founded in 753 B.C. Help children figure out how many candles would belong on a birthday cake baked for this occasion.

APRIL 22 } Bicycle Cycle

Today in 1884, Thomas Stevens began the first bike trip around the world. It took him 2 years and 9 months. *If you started out today and took the same amount of time to follow his route, when would you finish? How old would you be then?*

APRIL 23 } Money Exchange

Today, people in Bermuda celebrate the anniversary of the Peppercorn Ceremony of 1816. This event marks the payment of one peppercorn to rent the Old State House. It's a good time to examine unconventional forms of money used around the world, such as salt, feathers, or shells. A helpful resource is the book *Money* by Joe Cribb.

APRIL 24 } ¡Muchas Gracias!

On or around this day, people in El Paso, Texas, celebrate the anniversary of the first Thanksgiving. In April, you ask? Yes! In 1598 after Spanish settler Juan de Oñate completed a difficult four-month journey across harsh terrain, he ordered a public feast of thanksgiving. Help children figure out by how many years this event predated the Pilgrim Thanksgiving of 1621. (23 years)

APRIL 25 | Inves-TAG-ations

On this day in 1901, New York became the first state to require automobiles to have license plates. So it's a good day for some license plate math. You might apply the pattern your state uses for license plate numbers (for example, 3 letters and 3 numerals) to help children figure out how many different combinations there could be. Or take a little trip to the school parking lot to look for interesting patterns in license plates, such as repeated numbers, palindromes, multiples, and so on.

APRIL 26 | Math Quake!

Today is Richter Scale Day. Sponsors of this event wish to bring attention to the work of Charles Francis Richter (1900–1985) on his birthday. Richter developed the earthquake magnitude rating scale that bears his name. Gather some Richter scale data on earthquakes from an almanac. Help children compare magnitudes, which are given in decimals such as 7.3 or 8.1. Where was the highest-magnitude earthquake last year?

APRIL 27 | Morse Math

Happy Birthday to Samuel F.B. Morse (1791–1872), the inventor of the telegraph code of dots and dashes. Display a chart of the Morse code (ask the librarian for help), and practice how to form words by combining the long and short sounds. Then have children use the code to spell number words or other math terms.

APRIL 29 | Laughing Matters

Today is Moment of Laughter Day! Take a brief pause during math class for some unrestrained belly laughing, guffawing, or chuckling. How many distinctly different kinds of laughter can children identify?

APRIL 30 | Math Honesty

Celebrate National Honesty Day by having children do self-evaluations of their progress in math. Ask them to write down three things they are good at in math and three things they know they need more work on. Consider including these statements in students' math portfolios.

MAY by the MONTH

One of the sweetest months, May means celebrating mothers and recalling the sacrifices of those who gave their lives in battle. During May, events invite us to sleep better, breathe easier, and keep our cars in good condition. May is also—

⊙ **Better Sleep Month**

This month, have children chart the number of hours they sleep each night. After each week, examine the data together to answer questions like these:

⊙ *How long is your typical night's sleep?*

⊙ *What is the longest night's sleep you got this week? The shortest?*

⊙ *Do you think you get enough sleep?*

⊙ **National Bike Month**

About five million people around the nation participate in events this month to promote the use of bicycles for recreation and transportation. For information about events in your area, visit http://www.bikeleague.org. In the meantime, bring in a bike of any size or design and challenge children to measure it in as many ways as they can: weight, diameter and circumference of wheels, height of frame, width of fender, distance between handlebars, and so on.

⊙ **National Salsa Month**

And you thought that ketchup was America's favorite condiment? Sales figures show that salsa has outpaced that other red stuff. This event celebrates over 50 years of *picante* sauce, a kind of salsa first manufactured in 1947. Make some *salsa fresca* or serve salsa as a dip for tortilla chips or fresh veggies this month. Or do a cost comparison of different brands of salsa available in your area. Which is the best buy?

AND, May is also—

☆ **Asian Pacific American Heritage Month**

☆ **Breathe Easy Month**

☆ **Creative Beginnings Month**

☆ **National Good Car-Keeping Month**

☆ **National Physical Fitness and Sports Month**

☆ **National Moving Month**

☆ **National Barbecue Month**

☆ **National Egg Month**

☆ **Personal History Awareness Month**

MAY by the WEEK

WEEK 1 — Conserve Water/Detect-a-Leak Week

Combine math and ecological awareness anytime this week.

- **Drip Detectives:** How often do children forget to turn off a water faucet? Such accidents can waste lots of water. Put a measuring cup under a drippy faucet in your classroom. See how long it takes to collect 1 cup of water. Then find a way to estimate how much water would be wasted in an hour or in a day.

- **Drain Restraint:** According to *50 Simple Things You Can Do to Save the Earth* by The Earth Works Group, a running faucet gives out 3–5 gallons of water per minute. That means you can easily use 5 gallons of water or more if you leave the water running while you brush your teeth. If you were to turn it off between wetting and rinsing your toothbrush, and rinsing out your mouth, you could save 5–8 gallons of water per brushing! Figure out how much water your whole class could save!

AND, the first week in May is also—
- ☆ **Bread Pudding Recipe Exchange Week**
- ☆ **Cartoon Art Appreciation Week**
- ☆ **National Pet Week**
- ☆ **National Wildflower Week**

WEEK 2 — National Transportation Week

What modes of transportation are there in your area? Which have children been on?

- **Transport:** Tally subway, bus, car, bike, trolley, ferry—how many means of transportation can students name? Compile a list. Then tally how many children have experienced each kind. Figure out the most and least common forms of transportation in your area. Which is the children's favorite? Least favorite?

- **Toy Car Race:** Create a simple racetrack in your classroom or on the playground. Make it long and straight, with barriers on either side. Invite each student to bring in a toy car for a distance race. Set rules such as: maximum length, 10 inches; maximum weight, 10 ounces; no power source (except kid power!); and so on. Hold preliminary trials in which 2 or 3 cars race to determine the greatest distance traveled with one good shove. Rank the distances traveled. Then have runoffs until you determine the car that traveled the farthest.

AND, the second week in May is also—
- ☆ **Universal Family Week**

WEEK 3 | International Pickle Week

Dills or sweets? Slices or spears? Get your class into a pickle this week!

⦿ **Pickle Paths:** Have children imagine that they will make a continuous path of pickle slices that goes from your classroom to the lunchroom. How many slices would it take? How many jars of pickle slices would children need to pickle the way? Create other silly pickle problems for groups to solve.

⦿ **Hold the Pickles!** Have children weigh a full jar of pickles. Then have them guess how much of the total weight is pickles, how much is pickle juice, and how much is the jar and lid. Drain the pickles and weigh them, the juice, and the empty jar and lid separately to verify their guesses.

AND, the third week in May is also—

☆ **Buckle Up America! Week**

☆ **National Emergency Medical Services (EMS) Week**

☆ **National Safe Boating Week**

☆ **Running and Fitness Week**

☆ **World Trade Week**

WEEK 4 | National Educational Bosses Week

As the school year winds down, it's time to appreciate the hard work that principals, superintendents, department coordinators, heads of schools, and other educational leaders do all year long.

⦿ **The Principal's Office:** Invite children to make up story problems that have to do with children, the principal, and math. For example: Marty was sent to the principal's office at 10:15 A.M. The principal saw him 15 minutes later, and lectured him for 10 minutes. What time was it when Marty left? (10:40 A.M.)

AND, the fourth week in May is also—

☆ **[part of the] Hawaii State Fair**

☆ **[part of the] Spoleto Festival USA in Charleston, South Carolina**

MAY by the DAY

MAY 1 | Laws and Order

It's Law Day today and has been since 1958. It's a day to appreciate the value of laws in helping society run fairly and in good order. Why not make it a day to look at some math laws, such as the Commutative Law of Addition [3 + 4 = 4 + 3], the Associative Law of Multiplication [(2 x 3) x 5 = 2 x (3 x 5)], or the Zero Law of Division [you can never divide by zero]. Brainstorm some math laws children know, along with examples of them.

MAY 2 | Streaks

On this day in 1939, New York Yankee great Lou Gehrig played in 2,130 consecutive baseball games. He'd played in every scheduled game since June 1, 1925. It took 57 years for his record to be broken—by Baltimore Oriole Cal Ripken, Jr. Check his home page at http://www.2131.com to find out his total. If students began some kind of streak today that lasted for 2,130 consecutive days, when would it end?

MAY 3 | Theatre Run

On this day in 1960, a musical called *The Fantastics* opened at the Sullivan Street Playhouse in New York City—and it's still playing! Have students figure out the length of this play's remarkable run. At a rate of 8 shows a week, how many times has it been performed?

MAY 4 | Weather Watchers

It's National Weather Observer's Day, an event that honors people who love to follow the weather. Have children focus on weather statistics today, such as high and low temperatures, wind direction and speed, humidity, amount and type of precipitation, sky conditions, time of sunrise and sunset, and so on. Gather the data firsthand; check the newspaper, almanac, and Internet sites; or plan a trip to a weather department at a local TV station or airport. You might spend some time reading thermometers or comparing Celsius and Fahrenheit temperature scales.

MAY 5 — Mexican Matemáticas

It's *Cinco de Mayo,* or May Fifth, the Mexican national holiday that honors the victory of Mexican troops over the invading French at the Battle of Puebla (1862). It's a good day to make a batch of Mexican sand clay. Cook 2 cups cornstarch, 4 cups dry sand, and 3 cups cold water in an electric skillet for 5–10 minutes, stirring constantly, until the clay is very thick. Then turn the clay onto a plate and cover it with a damp towel until cool. Use the clay to form beads, which children can string into patterns or use for counting and sorting. Do your counting in Spanish!

MAY 6 — Nursing Numbers

It's National Nurses Day, an event that honors the excellent work nurses do to help sick and injured people. Why not take a bandage survey today: How many children have on one bandage? No bandages? Two or more? After you gather the data and chart it, make another chart that shows where the bandages are located: on hands, feet, arms, legs, faces, or somewhere else. Are they plain bandages or ones with designs?

MAY 7 — Shadow Math

Today, people in Union City, New Jersey, celebrate Martin Z. Mollusk Day. If Martin, a hermit crab, sees his shadow at 11 A.M, they believe that summer will begin a week early. No shadow means that summer will come at its usual time. Try this experiment in your school yard. Select a student to be Martin Z. Mollusk. At 11 A.M, go outside and see if Martin sees his shadow. If so, determine when summer should begin according to this wacky legend.

MAY 8 — Socks' Day Off

Are you ready for No Socks Day? Well, today is your chance! If you aren't going to wear socks today, at least use them for some math fun! Try pair-up races *(Which team can pair off a jumble of mismatched socks first?),* sock tosses to practice number facts, or sock estimation activities *(How many socks can you hold in one hand? How many socks can you stuff into an empty sneaker? How much does a dry sock weigh? A wet sock? A sock filled with birdseed?).*

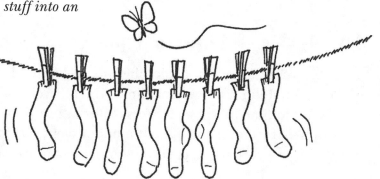

MAY 9   Postage Arrays

In 1936 postage stamps with different designs on a single sheet went on sale for the first time in New York City. Today, different-sized stamps come on sheets arranged in rectangular arrays: Some come in sheets of 20 stamps, 25 stamps, 32 stamps, 40 stamps, and so on. Have students draw a possible rectangular array for stamp sheets, and then calculate the total cost for the sheet at today's postage rates.

MAY 10   Benchmarks

On this day in 1931, a weather station in Burlington, New Jersey, reported hailstones the size of golf balls! Brainstorm with children objects in and around the classroom that are the approximate size of a golf ball, a tennis ball, a softball, a soccer ball, and so on. What other benchmarks can you use to estimate the size of spherical objects?

MAY 11   Eat-'Em-Up Math

It's Eat What You Want Day! Post a calorie list for foods children like to eat—and forget about balanced nutrition today. Include ice cream, cookies, soda, chips, and all that nasty stuff. Have children select the foods they'd want to eat today and determine the total number of calories they would consume if they did.

MAY 12   Math Limericks

It's Limerick Day, held on the birthday of English poet Edward Lear (1812–1888). Lear was best know for his light poems in this form. Why not have children work in groups to create one or more math limericks today? Here's one silly example:

> *There was a numerical hero,*
> *Whose job was to add on a zero.*
> *He made all the tens*
> *Into hundreds, my friends,*
> *So our dimes became dollars! Let's cheer-Oh!*

MAY 14   Time to Time

In 1862 Swiss inventor Adolphe Nicole patented the chronograph. This early kind of stopwatch finally let people time athletic events with great accuracy. Obtain a stopwatch today to time how long it takes children to complete certain tasks, such as writing the alphabet, completing a set of number facts, putting together a puzzle, opening a thick book to a certain page, and so on. Have children estimate first, then time the event.

MAY 16   The First Nickel

It's the anniversary of the U.S. nickel, which first appeared in 1866. That nickel, or five-cent-piece, had a shield on the front and the number 5 on the back. Today you might have children figure out how to express prices in numbers of nickels. Or examine fractions to recognize the fact that the nickel was *not* made entirely of nickel: it was one quarter nickel and three quarters copper. Find examples of regions or sets divided into fourths.

MAY 17   Merry-Go-Math

How old are merry-go-rounds? Well, historians report that the first merry-go-round appeared on this day at a fair in Turkey in 1620! It was powered by horses. Explore the merry-go-round on your school playground or in a local park. What is its diameter? Its circumference? How high off the ground is it? How many times will it go around after you let go? Is this affected by the number of people on it?

MAY 18   Eruption Patterns

On this date in 1980, Mount Saint Helens volcano in southwestern Washington State erupted. Steam and ash blew more than 11 miles into the sky. Its previous eruption took place in 1857. Have students figure out how many years there were between major eruptions (123). If this were a pattern, when would the next eruption of Mount Saint Helens take place? (in the year 2103)

MAY 19   Froggy Festivities

In 1928, 51 frogs entered the first frog-jumping jubilee in Calaveras County, California. The champion croaker jumped 3 feet 4 inches to beat all others. In May 1986, a modern champ made a record leap of 21 feet $5\frac{1}{2}$ inches, which, to date, has not yet been broken. Find the difference in length between those two jumps. (18 feet $1\frac{1}{2}$ in.) Or hold a froglike-jumping contest in your class. Entrants (students!) can line up on a starting line and take their best two-footed hop. Add extra points for most authentic croaking sounds! For more information, visit http://www.frogtown.org.

MAY 20 | Measurement Mania

It's the anniversary of the establishment of the International Bureau of Weights and Measures in 1875. Take time today to brainstorm a list of all the different units of weight and measure students can name.

MAY 21 | Fingerprint Facts

In 1934 Oskaloosa, Iowa, became the first American city to fingerprint each of its residents. Try a fingerprint activity in class today. Provide a stamp pad, ink, or paint with which students can make a set of prints of the fingers on one hand. Have groups examine the prints with hand lenses to look for loops, whorls, ridges, spirals, and so on. Children can classify the prints according to the patterns they detect.

MAY 22 | Sharing the Spoils

On this day in 1868, seven bold thieves robbed a train in a crime that is now known as the Great Train Robbery. They got away with $98,000 in cash! How much did each crook get if they shared the loot equally? ($14,000)

MAY 23 | Preschool Memories

In 1827 the nation's first nursery school opened in New York City. Survey the children in your class to find out at what age each child had his or her earliest school or day-care experience. Chart and display the results.

MAY 24 | Bridge the Gap

Happy Birthday to the Brooklyn Bridge! When this famed structure opened in 1883, it was the longest suspension bridge in the world—1,595 feet. Although it no longer holds any records for length, it still offers a way for cars to get between Brooklyn and Manhattan every day. Help children find the lengths of other bridges in the world and compare them. They can present this data in the form of a bar graph.

MAY 25 | Tap Patterns

It's National Tap Dance Day! This event is held on the birthday of one of America's great tap dancers, Bill "Bojangles" Robinson (1878–1949). Celebrate by inviting children to create tap patterns for classmates to repeat and extend.

MAY 26 \ Shuttle Math

Happy Birthday to Sally Ride (b. 1951), America's first woman in space. Her historic mission on the shuttle Challenger STS-7 took off on June 18, 1983, and returned to Earth 146 hours 24 minutes later. *How many days long was Ride's ride?* (just over 6 days) *What was the date of her return?* (June 24)

MAY 27 \ Golden Gate Towers

Today in 1937, the Golden Gate Bridge, which links the city of San Francisco with Marin County to the north, was dedicated and opened to traffic. Since then it has become one of San Francisco's most famous landmarks. Its towers, which often poke through the famed Bay Area fog, stand 745 feet above the water and are the tallest bridge towers in the world. Help students figure out how this height compares to the height of buildings in your area or about how many stories high the towers are.

MAY 28 \ High Fives

Happy Birthday to Marie, Cecile, Yvonne, Emile, and Annette Dionne, the world's first set of quintuplets to survive infancy. These famous Canadian babies were born on this day in 1934 near Callender, Ontario. Today, have children think of things that customarily come in groups of 5, such as basketball teams and fingers.

MAY 29 \ Mountain Math

On this day in 1953, New Zealand explorer Sir Edmund Hillary and Tenzing Norgay, his Sherpa guide, became the first team known to reach the top of Mount Everest in Nepal. Everest, the world's tallest mountain, rises 29,029 feet (8,848 meters) above sea level. Help children figure out about how many miles tall it is. (about $5\frac{1}{2}$ miles)

JUNE by the MONTH

Weddings, Father's Day, the start of summer, the end of school—all are key June events. But that's not everything. June is also—

⊙ **Dairy Month**

Milk this event for all the math it holds! This might be a good time to keep a dairy diary, in which students record all dairy products they consume for a week. You might also examine the lunchroom menus this month to see how many main courses include dairy products. Students can chart or graph the information, make calorie or protein charts, or calculate costs-per-serving for some dairy products, such as a half-gallon of ice cream or a quart of milk.

⊙ **National Iced Tea Month**

This beverage has become so popular that it rates its own national month! What kinds of iced tea do your students drink? Sweetened or unsweetened? Plain or flavored? From a mix, fresh-brewed, or out of a can or bottle? Poll the group. Then brainstorm with the class to list questions to research and answer about iced tea. For instance:

> ⊙ *How long does it take an ice cube to melt in a glass of hot tea?*
>
> ⊙ *How much tea can you pour into an iced-tea glass that is full of ice?*
>
> ⊙ *How many servings can you make with 1 cup of iced tea mix?*

⊙ **Vision Research Month**

This might be a good time to explore optical illusions and other designs and patterns that attempt to fool the eye. Display some works by Dutch artist M. C. Escher, and consult resources for puzzles and activities involving shapes-within-shapes, parts of a whole, mirror images, cube patterns, symmetry, creative bisecting, and so on. One good source is *Critical Thinking Activities* by Dale Seymour and Ed Beardslee (Dale Seymour Publications).

AND, June is also—

☆ **Fireworks Safety Month**   ☆ **National Roving With Rover Month**

☆ **National Accordion Awareness Month**   ☆ **National Safety Month**

☆ **National Beef-Steak Month**

June by the Week

National Fishing Week

Give your math classes a new angle this week with projects related to fishing.

⊚ **Weight and Strength:** Obtain samples of different kinds of fishing line, which is rated by how much weight it can hold without snapping. Have children examine the pieces to look for similarities and differences. Then have them test each piece by tying on different weights.

⊚ **Fish Tales:** Rumor has it that people exaggerate the size of a "fish that got away." Challenge children to snag a tall tale when they hear one. Prepare an assortment of statements that include math measures; make some reasonable, others exaggerated. Read each statement aloud, asking students to distinguish the ones that make sense from the ones that are outlandish. Have children explain their thinking.

AND, the first week in June is also—

☆ **International Volunteers Week**

☆ **Small Business Week**

☆ **Stepparents' Week**

National Flag Week

Use Old Glory to glorify math lessons anytime this week.

⊚ **Flag Fractions:** Have groups examine the flag to describe it in terms of fractions. For instance, they might notice that $\frac{7}{13}$ of the stripes are red and $\frac{6}{13}$ are white, or that the blue field takes up about $\frac{1}{4}$ of the flag.

⊚ **Fly Time:** By tradition, places that display the American flag raise it at sunrise and lower it at sundown. Challenge children to determine how long the flag will fly this month if it is raised every day at sunrise and taken down every evening at sunset. They can consult an almanac or newspaper for daily sunrise and sunset times.

AND, the second week in June is also—

☆ **National Ergonomics week**

☆ **National Headache Awareness Week**

☆ **National Hug Holiday Week**

☆ **National Little League Baseball Week**

☆ **Pet Appreciation Week**

WEEK 3 | National Clay Week Festival

"Knead" new math plans? Think of Uhrichsville, Ohio, which hosts this annual event to honor the area as the Clay Center of the World. Here are some ideas.

⊚ **Math by the Slice:** Have children create cubes of modeling clay. Challenge them to visualize the geometric shape of the face they would reveal if they sliced all the way through the cube at different angles. Provide unbent paper clips as slicing wires, and have groups make different cuts. Have children predict what they think they'll see and sketch what they do see.

⊚ **Math Models:** Have children make clay models of different geometric solids. They can display each model along with a sign that states its properties, such as number of faces, edges, and vertices; length, width, and height; or how to find its volume or surface area.

AND, the third week in June is also—

☆ **National Hermit Week**

☆ **Radio Talk Show Week**

WEEK 4 | Assistant Principal's Week

As the school year winds down, interview the vice-principal for a math activity.

⊚ **Comparing Heads:** Have children gather statistics about the principal and the assistant principal, such as height, number of years' teaching experience, number of years at your school, and so on. Have pairs create comparing questions about the two. Pairs can exchange and solve each other's problems.

AND, the fourth week in June is also—

☆ **Amateur Radio Week**

☆ **Carpenter Ant Awareness Week**

☆ **Deaf-Blindness Awareness Week**

☆ **Universal Father's Week**

JUNE by the DAY

JUNE 1) Perimeter Perambulation

On this day in 1908, John Krohn began walking the perimeter of the 48 contiguous United States while pushing a wheelbarrow. It took him 357 days (but he never walked on Sundays) to walk 9,024 miles. He went through 11 pairs of shoes, 112 pairs of socks, and 5 wheels for his barrow. In Krohn's honor, challenge children to use a trundle wheel to find the perimeter of your classroom, lunchroom, playground, ball field, or other large space. If you don't have a trundle wheel, children can use string or measuring tapes to accomplish the same task.

JUNE 3) Geography Anomaly

Happy Mount Chimborazo Day. This event is to inform people that Ecuador's Mount Chimborazo pokes farther into space than any other mountain on Earth. Chimborazo (20,561 feet) is located near the equator. Due to our planet's bulging shape, it is 13 miles farther from the center of the earth to sea level at the equator than it is at the North Pole. So, by this geographic measure, Mount Everest is taller (29,029 feet), but Chimborazo sticks out farther. Have children locate Chimborazo on a map or globe, and determine how much shorter it is than Everest. (8,468 feet)

JUNE 5) Angle Attitudes

It's National Attitude Day! Turn this event into an excuse to study angles. Demonstrate how to use the corner of an index card as a model of a right angle (90°). Or have older children learn to use a protractor to find angle measures. Using either tool, they can also find examples of classroom objects with an attitude (angle measure) of more than 90° or less than 90°.

JUNE 6) Screen Sizes

In 1933 in Camden, New Jersey, the first drive-in movie theatre opened. People arrived in their cars to see films on a gigantic outdoor screen. That first screen was 40 feet wide and 50 feet tall! Have children measure the dimensions of screens they customarily watch: television screens, computer screens, classroom movie screens, and so on. Students can record the information they find on labeled sketches or on charts. Older students can compare screen sizes by area.

94

JUNE 7 ❭ Novel Pricing

In 1860 Mrs. Ann Stevens published *Malaeska, The Indian Wife of the White Hunter.* This 128-page novel sold for ten cents, making it the first "dime novel." Have children find out the average price of a novel today (paperback or hardback) and compare the prices. About how many times more expensive is a novel today?

JUNE 8 ❭ Postal Problems

In 1872 the United States Congress authorized use of the penny postcard. This innovation created a way to send a mail message for less than the cost of a regular letter. Find out the cost of mailing a postcard today. Describe the rate of increase. For older students, you can pose postcard/letter postage problems like this: *If you had $5 to spend on letter stamps and postcard stamps, how many different combinations of each could you buy?*

JUNE 9 ❭ Duck Math

Happy Birthday, Donald Duck! The illustrious quacker was "born" in 1934. How old is Donald today? How long do real ducks usually live?

JUNE 10 ❭ Portuguese Area

Today is a national holiday in Portugal to honor its national poet, Luis Vas de Camoes (1524–1580). It's a good day to point out Portugal on the map. Tell students that the area of Portugal is 35,456 square miles. Challenge them to look through an almanac to find an American state a little smaller than Portugal and another that's somewhat larger. Then have them determine the difference in area between Portugal and those states. (Maine, at 35,387 square miles, is 69 square miles smaller; Indiana, at 36,420 square miles, is 964 square miles larger.)

JUNE 11 ❭ Hot Dog Units

On this day in 1939, the King and Queen of England came to lunch at the White House. President Franklin Roosevelt served them the most all-American food he could think of—hot dogs! Here's a new use for this picnic treat—as a measuring tool! How many dogs long and wide is your classroom? First guess, then figure out a way to calculate it exactly.

JUNE 12   Sizzling Surface

On this day in 1967, the Russian space agency launched Veneer 4, an instrument capsule that eventually landed on the planet Venus and recorded a temperature of 536°F. Phew!! How much hotter was it on Venus that day than it is in your community today?

JUNE 13   Niners!

On this day in 1971 in a hospital in Sydney, Australia, Geraldine Broderick gave birth to nine babies: five boys and four girls. (Unfortunately, none of the tiny infants survived longer than six days.) Challenge children to figure out the word for nine babies born at once. (nonuplets) Think of other things that usually come in nines, such as baseball teams and innings in a baseball game.

JUNE 14   Math 200

As of today, there are exactly 200 days left in the year. Challenge students to list as many different ways as they can to express the quantity 200. For instance, they can write it in Roman numerals (CC), as an addition fact (150 + 50), as a multiplication fact (50 x 4), or as a statement (the number of pennies in $2).

JUNE 15   Trombones on Parade

On this day in 1984, American composer Meredith Willson died. He was best known for his Broadway show *The Music Man*. One of its most popular songs is "76 Trombones." Honor Willson's memory by playing that song for the class, and invite those who know the words to sing along. Then challenge groups to figure out various ways for 76 trombone players to march in a parade in equal rows.

JUNE 17   Survey of Champions

On this day in 1870, George Cormack created Wheaties cereal, the "Breakfast of Champions." Take a poll to find out children's favorite cold breakfast cereals. Predict the winners. Then post the results in graph form.

JUNE 18   Whole-Hog Spending

It's National Splurge Day! Sponsors of this event encourage people to go out and do something indulgent. Invite children to think about what they would splurge on if they could spend money in any way they wanted. Classify the splurge purchases by category, or as cheap, medium, expensive, or over-the-top.

JUNE 19 | A Cat's Age

Happy Birthday to Garfield, that lasagna-loving cartoon cat. Jim Davis published the first Garfield comic strip on this day in 1978. Have children find Garfield's age. How long do most real cats live? How does this fact compare with Garfield's age?

JUNE 20 | State Rankings

On this day in 1863, West Virginia became our thirty-fifth state. As of 1998 West Virginia ranked as the thirty-fifth state in terms of population. Provide almanacs, social studies books, or other resources with information about states in terms of admission, area, and population. Challenge students to find another state whose rankings match in two categories. (As of 1998 Texas ranked second in population and in area.)

JUNE 21 | LP Math

On this day in 1948, Dr. Peter Goldmark of the Columbia Broadcasting System introduced the LP, or long-playing vinyl record. This 12-inch "platter" could hold 23 minutes of music on each side, which was a great improvement over earlier records. Compile a list of students' favorite popular songs with their play lengths. Suppose you wanted to put out an album with all the songs on the class list. How many records would you need in the album?

JUNE 22 | Voting Age

On this day in 1970, President Richard Nixon signed into law the Twenty-Sixth Amendment to the U.S. Constitution. This amendment lowered the voting age across the nation to 18 years of age. Challenge students to figure out how long it will be until they may cast their first official vote in a public election and how long it will be until they can vote in a presidential election.

JUNE 24 | Teddy Bear Tally

On this day in 1995, the Dublin Zoo in Ireland held the world's largest teddy bear picnic: 33,573 teddy bears and their owners were there! If your class held a teddy bear picnic, how many teddy bears would your students be able to bring?

JUNE 25   Musical Math

Today is International Sing-Out Day. Sponsors of this worldwide event encourage you to participate by singing your words instead of saying them or by breaking into song like characters in musicals do. Apply this idea to your math classes today by singing out directions and by encouraging students to respond musically to you!

JUNE 26   International Members

On this day in 1945, representatives of 50 nations of the world got together in San Francisco to sign the charter for the United Nations. Find out how many nations belong to the U.N. today to figure out how many more member nations there are now.

JUNE 27   Population Comparison

Happy Freedom Day to the African nation of Djibouti. Find Djibouti on a map or globe. On this day in 1977, Djibouti gained its independence from France. As of 1996 the population of Djibouti was 434,116. Challenge children to find the U.S. state that is closest in population to it. Find the difference in the populations. (At 481,400, Wyoming is the state whose population is closest; the difference is 47,284.)

JUNE 29   Frisbee Flings

On this day in 1985 in La Mirada, California, Judy Horowitz set the women's record for the throw, run, and catch of a Frisbee. The distance was 196 feet 11 inches. Have an outdoor Frisbee-throwing contest with your students. Mark off a start line, and measure how far each child can fling a Frisbee.

JUNE 30   Balancing Act

In 1859 Charles Blondin became the first person to cross over Niagara Falls on a tightrope. But don't try this at school. Instead, have children attempt to keep their balance while walking a chalk line, a tile crack, or a rope set out on the ground. Measure how far they can go without losing their balance or missing the line.

SUMMER STOCK (JULY/AUGUST)

MONTH OF JULY
Inventive Minds

July is Anti-Boredom Month! Celebrate by trying never to be bored this month. You might invent a math game, create an interesting and original math design, or send a hard story problem to your teacher. You might see how fast you can count to 100, how far you can throw a ball, or how high you can jump.

JULY 1 | Zoo-ology

On this day in 1874, the Philadelphia Zoological Society welcomed its first visitor to America's first zoo. On opening day, 3,000 visitors came to see the 1,000 animals on display. Admission was 25 cents for adults and 10 cents for children. *At those rates, how much would your entire family spend to go to the zoo? How do these rates compare to today's rates at the zoo nearest to your community?*

JULY 1 | Halfway Day

Noon today marks the halfway point of the year (unless this is a leap year, in which case midnight tomorrow is Halfway Day). Identify the halfway point in some of your favorite activities. For instance: *When is your half-birthday? When is halfway between Halloweens? When is the halfway point in your favorite song? Your favorite movie? Your favorite TV show? Your favorite meal?*

JULY 3 | Shady Math

It's Stay Out of the Sun Day today. Sponsors of this event hope to remind you of the importance of using sunscreen to protect your skin from harmful ultraviolet rays. The SPF number on sunscreen estimates how long you can stay in the sun before you burn. So an SPF of 8 means you can stay in the sun 8 times longer than you could without the sunscreen. *How long could you safely stay in the sun if you'd normally burn in 5 minutes but you smear on some SPF 15?* (75 minutes)

JULY 7) Baseball Toss

Happy Birthday to Satchel Paige (1906?–1982), Baseball Hall of Fame pitcher who was the first African American pitcher to play in the American League. How far can you throw a baseball? First estimate, then try it and measure. You can measure in standard units, such as feet or meters, or mark off the throw in steps or paces. Chart the results of ten throws to see if you notice any patterns.

JULY 11) Pet Pictures

It's All-American Pet Photo Day! Celebrate by taking pictures of your pet sleeping, playing, eating, or just being cute. Or pose your pet in a silly costume before you snap the shutter. Figure out how much wood you would need to make a frame for your favorite photo or how much it would cost to frame the best three snapshots.

JULY 20) Moon Math

On this day in 1969, Neil Armstrong and Edwin "Buzz" Aldrin landed the lunar module Eagle on the surface of the moon. This milestone marked the first time humans ever landed on the moon. They got there at 4:17 P.M. and stayed for 21 hours and 36 minutes. *When did they leave?* (1:53 P.M. the next day)

JULY 24) Relative Figures

It's Cousins Day! You can celebrate by writing letters to all your cousins, calling them on the phone (if your folks give the OK!), sending them e-mail, or at least making a list of all of them. Then find the total age of all your cousins. Extend by finding out how many years of relatives you have.

FIRST WEEK of AUGUST
Clowning Around

It's International Clown Week! Celebrate by painting a symmetrical design on your face or on a friend's face. Describe your designs. Complete the day by trying to learn to juggle, to walk on stilts, to do a handstand, or to do a magic trick.

AUGUST 5 — Allowance Tax

On this day in 1861, President Abraham Lincoln signed a law creating the first federal income tax, which took effect on January 1 of the next year. People had to pay three cents out of every dollar they earned. At that rate, figure out the tax you would have to pay on your allowance this month.

AUGUST 9 — Math Reading

It's Book Lovers Day! Celebrate by reading a book that has a math theme, such as *For Alexander Who Was Rich Last Sunday* or *The Doorbell Rang*. Or try a biography of a mathematician, such as Benjamin Bannecker or Albert Einstein, or any book that has a number, a shape word, or a measurement word in the title.

AUGUST 12 — Tugging Time

The longest tug-of-war ever held took place in India on this day in 1889. There were no official time limits back then, so the teams tugged for 2 hours 41 minutes before one team finally won. How long will it take you and some of your friends to out-tug another team? Get two teams, a sturdy rope, a stopwatch, and give it a try!

AUGUST 13 — Math with Hitch

Happy Birthday to movie director Sir Alfred Hitchcock (1899–1980). One of his great suspense films is called *The Thirty-Nine Steps*. *How far would 39 walking steps take you? What if you took baby steps? Giant steps?* Guess, then find out!

AUGUST 15 — Mellow Measures

It's National Relaxation Day today. Celebrate by taking the time to relax: curl up with a good book, sip a big glass of lemonade, watch a favorite video, take your dog on a long walk, or take a bubble bath. *How many hours of rest would you like? How does that number compare with the amount of rest you usually get?*

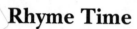
Rhyme Time

etry Day! Invite some friends over and make up silly poems, ridiculous
s, and frivolous verses. *How many words can you list that rhyme with* math?

AUGUST 26 | **Noise Estimates**

On this day in 1883, the Indonesian volcanic island of Krakatoa erupted. The mighty
explosion, which created tidal waves and hurled rock fragments 50 miles into the air,
was heard 3,000 miles away! If Krakatoa had been in your vicinity, figure out some
places about 3,000 miles away that might have heard its sound.